Cyberpayments and Money Laundering

Problems and Promise

*Roger C. Molander, David A. Mussington,
Peter A. Wilson*

Critical Technology Institute

RAND
A NATIONAL RESOURCE
1948–1998

The research described in this report was conducted by RAND's Critical Technologies Institute.

ISBN: 0-8330-2616-X

Published 1998 by RAND
1700 Main Street, P.O. Box 2138, Santa Monica, CA 90407-2138
1333 H St., N.W., Washington, D.C. 20005-4707
RAND URL: http://www.rand.org/
To order RAND documents or to obtain additional information, contact Distribution Services: Telephone: (310) 451-7002; Fax: (310) 451-6915; Internet: order@rand.org

RAND

Cyberpayments and Money Laundering

Problems and Promise

Roger C. Molander, David A. Mussington, Peter A. Wilson

Prepared for the
Office of Science and Technology Policy and
Financial Crimes Enforcement Network

Critical Technology Institute

PREFACE

This report summarizes research performed by RAND for the Financial Crimes Enforcement Network (FinCEN) of the U.S. Department of the Treasury as part of FinCEN's overall effort to examine potential money laundering concerns raised by the deployment of Cyberpayment systems.

This study was undertaken in recognition that law enforcement and regulatory authorities will likely be confronted with new challenges in conducting their traditional oversight of the financial services industry and in investigating illicit financial activity. The growth of electronic commerce presents a new opportunity for criminals to commit fraud and abuse against business firms and consumers. Law enforcement authorities and payment system regulators similarly confront a rapidly changing set of payment technologies that may serve to undermine traditional investigative methods for detecting fraud and abuse.

This report should be of special interest to those who are exploring the effects of the information revolution on the nature of crime. It should also be of interest to analysts and observers of electronic commerce concerned with the future evolution of regulatory and law enforcement responses to the information revolution.

The purpose of this report and RAND's research was to explore with the public and private sector the potential vulnerabilities of new payment technologies to abuse by money launderers and other financial criminals. This report is not intended to provide recommendations to either detect or prevent such illicit uses of these systems. Indeed, while these systems are still under development, it would be premature to do so. Rather, this study was designed to foster a constructive dialogue between law enforcement, financial regulators, and the financial services industry so that they are able to take steps to guard against illicit uses of cyberpayment systems as these systems begin to gain acceptance in the financial marketplace.

The research reported here was accomplished within the Critical Technologies Institute (CTI). CTI was created in 1991 by an act of Congress. It is a federally funded research and development center operated by RAND. CTI's mission is to:

- Help improve public policy by conducting objective, independent research and analysis to support the Office of Science and Technology Policy in the Executive Office of the President of the United States;
- Help decisionmakers understand the likely consequences of their decisions and choose among alternative policies; and
- Improve understanding in both the public and private sectors of the ways in which technological efforts can better serve national objectives.

CTI research focuses on problems of science and technology policy that involve or affect multiple Executive Branch agencies, different branches of the U.S. Government, or interaction between the U.S. government and states, other nations, or the private sector.

Inquiries regarding CTI or this document may be directed to:

Bruce Don
Director, Critical Technologies Institute
RAND
1333 H St., N.W.
Washington, D.C. 20005
Phone: (202) 296-5000
Web: http:/www.rand.org/cti
Email: cti@rand.org

CONTENTS

FIGURES

TABLES

SUMMARY

PURPOSE AND APPROACH OF THIS REPORT

Background

Cyberpayments are an emerging new class of instruments and payment systems that support the electronic transfer of value. These transfers may take place via networks, such as the Internet, or through the use of stored value-type smart cards. Because of the efficiency and ease with which they transfer value, these systems may also present new challenges to law enforcement. Technology exists which could permit these systems to combine the speed of the present bank-based wire transfer systems with the anonymity of currency. As a result, there are issues that must be addressed as these systems are being developed to ensure the prevention and detection of money laundering and other illegal financial transactions.

The Financial Crimes Enforcement Network (FinCEN), an agency of the U.S. Department of the Treasury, sought RAND's assistance as part of an overall effort to examine potential money laundering concerns raised by the deployment of Cyberpayment systems. In furtherance of this general objective, FinCEN supports an extensive ongoing dialogue with the Cyberpayments industry.

FinCEN's first step in advancing this dialogue took place in September 1995, when it conducted a Cyberpayments Colloquium at the New York University School of Law. The Colloquium brought together financial services providers, software developers, academics, consumer representatives, and regulatory, policy, and law enforcement officials to discuss advances in the design and implementation of emerging electronic payment systems. In addition, in May 1996, FinCEN, in cooperation with the National Defense University, hosted a computer-based cyber-money laundering simulation exercise in which the participants used advanced decision making techniques to create hypothetical Cyberpayment-based money laundering scenarios.

Cyberpayment systems have also been a topic of interest to the White House, the United States Congress and various other law enforcement and regulatory agencies. In July 1997, the President released a report on the Global Information Infrastructure (GII), entitled "A Framework for Global Electronic Commerce," a portion of which directly addressed Cyberpayment issues. In addition, Cyberpayment systems were the subject of hearings conducted in 1996 by the Subcommittee on Domestic and International Monetary Policy of the House Banking and Financial Services Committee.

Internationally, Cyberpayment systems have also received extensive attention. Multilateral discussions and studies have been undertaken by both the G-7's Financial Action Task Force (FATF) and the G-10's Working Party On Electronic Money. In June 1996, a new recommendation #13 was added to the FATF's 40 Recommendations. It states that "[c]ountries should pay special attention to money laundering threats inherent in new or developing technologies that may favor anonymity, and take measures, if needed, to prevent their use in money laundering schemes."

The RAND Effort

To address FinCEN's interest in this emerging area, RAND designed, conducted and analyzed a strategic decision-making exercise directed at both the potential problems and opportunities that the emergence of Cyberpayment systems pose for U.S. and global anti-money laundering efforts.

This report presents a description and findings of that exercise. These findings reflect the widely divergent views expressed by the participants and are based on conclusions from research RAND performed independently. The report also identifies potential alternative law enforcement and regulatory approaches to address patterns of Cyberpayment system misuse. The report reaches two basic conclusions: first, if sufficient precautionary measures are not considered while these systems develop, Cyberpayment systems could have the potential to undermine current law enforcement strategies for combating illegal money laundering; and second, this issue must be viewed as international in scope, necessitating governments to collaborate in formulating new strategies to counter any potential money laundering threats.

The overall conclusions expressed in this report are those of the RAND Corporation and do not necessarily reflect the positions of FinCEN or the U.S. Department of the Treasury.

The Exercise

This summary presents the results of the exercise's four principal tasks:

1. Describe current Cyberpayment concepts and systems.
2. Identify an initial set of Cyberpayment characteristics of particular concern to law enforcement with respect to money laundering.
3. Identify major issues Cyberpayment policies will need to address to guard against abuse by money launderers.
4. Provide alternate approaches to address potential Cyberpayment system abuse in a set of potential action plans.

Participants in the exercise included a range of representatives from the Executive Branch, the Cyberpayments industry, the banking industry, the Congress, and academia. Responses to potential Cyberpayment misuse were compiled through recording the exercise experiences of participants, and through observation and analysis of dilemmas posed by the scenario itself. During this process, traditional law enforcement and regulatory measures were compared to the potentially new challenges posed by Cyberpayment technologies. The extensive participation of Cyberpayment industry representatives made it possible to gain a working knowledge of the rapidly evolving state of the art.

Because of the challenge of educating exercise participants about both Cyberpayments and money laundering, the exercise was built on a familiar framework - drug cartels and money laundering. The hypothesis was that Mexican drug cartels would become early adopters of Cyberpayments for money laundering. The time frame for the scenario was intended to be far enough into the future (2004) so that Cyberpayment systems would have progressed substantially, but not to the point where the market and technology for such systems had fully matured.

In support of this scenario, a "future history" was developed that described: (1) hypothetical developments in Cyberpayment systems; (2) the emergence of criminal exploitation of Cyberpayment systems for money laundering; (3) international and U.S. responses to this challenge; and (4) hypothetical drug cartel exploitation of Mexican Cyberpayment systems for money laundering in the context of a Mexican drug war.

TRADITIONAL MONEY LAUNDERING PROCESSES

In most financial transactions, there is a financial trail to link the funds to the person(s) involved. Criminals avoid using traditional payment systems, such as checks, credit cards, etc., because of this paper trail. They prefer to use cash because it is anonymous. Physical cash, however, has some disadvantages. It is bulky and difficult to move. For example, 44 pounds of cocaine, worth $1 million equals 256 pounds of street cash worth $1 million. The street cash is more than six times the weight of the drugs. The existing payment systems and cash are both problems for criminals. Even more so for large transnational organized crime groups. Regulations and banking controls have increased costs and risks.

The physical movement of large quantities of cash is the money launderer's biggest problem. To better understand the potential for abuse of Cyberpayment systems to launder money, a brief explanation of how criminals "legitimize" cash through the traditional money laundering process is provided.

Placement, *layering* and *integration* are terms used by law enforcement to describe the three stages through which criminal proceeds are laundered.

Placement. Placement is the first stage in the money laundering process and it is when illegal proceeds are most vulnerable to detection. It is during the placement stage that physical currency enters the financial system. When illicit monies are deposited at a financial institution, placement has occurred. The purchase of money orders using cash from a criminal enterprise is another example of placement. The Bank Secrecy Act (BSA) and related regulations mandate the reporting of certain types of financial transactions which involve cash and/or certain monetary instruments. To conceal their activities money launderers must either circumvent the legitimate financial system entirely, or violate reporting/record-keeping rules established under the BSA. Accordingly, law enforcement officials, working in cooperation with the financial industry, are in a unique position to combat money laundering during this stage.

Layering. Layering describes an activity intended to obscure the trail which is left by "dirty" money. During the layering stage, a launderer may conduct a series of financial transactions in order to build layers between the funds and their illicit source. For example, a series of bank-to-bank funds transfers would constitute layering. Activities of this nature, particularly when they involve funds transfers between tax haven and bank secrecy jurisdictions, can make it very difficult for investigators to follow the trail of money.

Integration. During the final stage in the laundering process, illicit funds are integrated with monies from legitimate commercial activities as they enter the mainstream economy. The illicit funds thus take on the appearance of legitimacy. The integration of illicit monies into a legitimate economy is very difficult to detect unless an audit trail had been established during the placement or layering stages.

THE CURRENT STATE OF CYBERPAYMENT TECHNOLOGY

Progress toward technical and commercial standards in the Cyberpayment industry has been steady and the emergence of Cyberpayment systems is gathering momentum. At present, a small number of stored-value type smart card and network-based products are undergoing pilot testing. These tests are taking place on a global basis, thus underscoring the international nature of the emerging Cyberpayments infrastructure.

Some Cyberpayment instrument features such as peer-to-peer value transfer and payer anonymity offer to the consumer an instrument with much of the flexibility and convenience of cash together with an enhanced ability to conduct purchases on an almost global basis. This technology suggests that law enforcement must begin to consider the potential implications of an environment where the wide availability of Cyberpayment instruments could substantially reduce the use of physical currency in consumer-level transactions. The features of Cyberpayment instruments that deliver this new functionality are discussed in the next chapter.

In considering the potential Cyberpayments-money laundering nexus, it should be noted that the same technologies underlying Cyberpayment products could also be used as new information gathering tools by law enforcement and payment system regulators. The privacy implications of enhanced government surveillance of information networks is an issue that was addressed at considerable length during the exercise. Any policies in this area would have to be carefully crafted so as to meet constitutional protections of individual privacy and governmental concerns with critical infrastructure protection.

THE POTENTIAL EXPLOITATION OF CYBERPAYMENT SYSTEMS FOR MONEY LAUNDERING

The RAND exercise focused on identifying potential characteristics in Cyberpayment systems that could be exploited by money launderers. By their nature, Cyberpayment systems have the potential to eliminate the money launderer's biggest problem, the physical movement of large amounts of cash. The globalization of many proposed Cyberpayment systems may also offer money launderers opportunities to exploit national differences in security standards and oversight rules to conceal the movement of illicit funds.

Previous forums such as the Financial Action Task Force (FATF) have identified a number of features that law enforcement must consider with respect to Cyberpayment transactions. Among them are (1) Disintermediation; (2) A Potential Wide Variety of Cyberpayment Service Providers; (3) Peer-to-Peer Transfers; (4) Transaction Anonymity and; (5) Denomination Limits and Expiration Dates. Each of these basic features is described in more detail below. While these basic features make Cyberpayments attractive as a potential means to reduce transaction costs in commerce and contribute to the increased efficiency of payment methods, these features are also consistent with existing vulnerabilities that have been exploited by criminals conducting financial transactions using traditional means.

Disintermediation. Historically, law enforcement and regulatory officials have relied on the intermediation of banks and other regulated financial institutions to provide "choke points" through which funds must generally pass and where records would be maintained. Disintermediation involves the transfer of financial value between entities without the intermediate involvement of an identifiable third party subject to governmental oversight (e.g., record-keeping requirements via a bank). Should Cyberpayment systems permit disintermediated value transfers in unlimited amounts, money launderers could use this as an opportunity to avoid traditional law enforcement money tracing methods.

Potential Wide Variety of Cyberpayment Service Providers. Bank and non-bank entities may be subject to different rules regarding their operation of Cyberpayment systems. This difference is already the case in several nations where non-bank Cyberpayment issuers are currently subject to a different set of rules from banks. A simple extension of traditional payment system oversight to new non-bank Cyberpayment issuers may address some of the concerns regarding potential system abuse by money launderers. However, the new systems are configured differently and constantly mutating, so a "one size fits all" regulatory approach is not necessarily appropriate or even possible.

Peer-To-Peer Transfers of Value. Some Cyberpayment systems allow consumers to transfer value peer-to-peer (and thus, disintermediated) using an electronic "wallet," a telephone, or via the Internet. Such value transfers pose perhaps the most direct challenge to governmental oversight of Cyberpayment systems. In the absence of intelligence information or evidence from non-Cyberpayment system sources (e.g., physical surveillance) triggering an investigation into specific suspect stored value instrument activity, clearly illicit or suspicious peer-to-peer transfers of value are unlikely to be detected.

Transaction Anonymity. In some emerging Cyberpayment products, the origins of funds are relatively opaque and the identity of the individual or entity transferring them difficult to determine. In fact, payer anonymity (the identity of the party initiating a Cyberpayment value transfer) is a central characteristic of some proposed systems. For Cyberpayment value transfers (e.g., via the Internet or the basic telephone system), transaction anonymity could be an almost insuperable barrier to law enforcement detection. While candidate solutions for this problem have been put forward, they raise issues concerning individual privacy.

Denomination Limits and Expiration Dates. Cyberpayment product issuers are likely to limit the maximum amounts that can be stored on smart cards or other devices, to reduce the risks of fraud or other losses. As with credit cards, Cyberpayment issuers will also likely establish needs-based denomination limits that would be determined by commercial and market factors. (Recent consumer tests of Cyberpayment systems indicate likely consumer limits of approximately $1,000 - $3,000). Cyberpayment products held by retailers are likely to have a much larger value limit than those for most individuals and differ widely between retailers. Cyberpayment value could also be programmed to expire after a certain number of transfers. As early technology adopters, money launderers could be expected to exploit whatever limits are established, just as they do now by structuring transactions under currency reporting limits, obtaining multiple cards (credit or debit), using multiple names, or employing multiple issuers.

THE EXERCISES

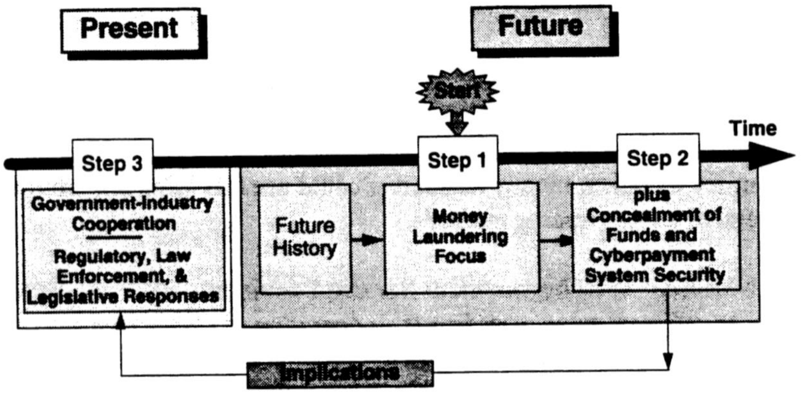

Figure 1. Exercise Methodology

The first two steps of the exercise (see Figure 1) were set in the year 2004. The time frame for the exercise was intended to be far enough in the future so that Cyberpayment systems would have progressed substantially. The third step returned to the present or, more precisely, the very near future. The basic steps of the exercise were:

STEP ONE. First phase of the crisis. Competing Mexican and Colombian drug traffickers increasingly exploit Cyberpayment technologies for money laundering. U.S. decision-makers face a series of difficult tactical and strategic issues in the areas of law enforcement, international financial institution collaboration, and bilateral initiatives to improve U.S.-Mexican Cyberpayment system oversight.

The participants were asked to consider, debate and select appropriate tactical responses to the emerging crisis.

STEP TWO. Second phase of the crisis. Escalation in the "Mexican Drug War" and further exploitation of Cyberpayment systems for money laundering by the drug cartels, in spite of more aggressive law enforcement efforts. Cartel efforts threaten the financial and perhaps political stability of Mexico.

The participants discovered that Mexico was in the middle of a financial crisis, that the new Cyberpayment system had a flawed encryption scheme and that Mexican drug cartels were taking advantage of the situation. By laundering money, the cartels were causing major economic and price destabilization through manipulating Cyberpayment systems. As the Mexican crisis escalated to the point where money was flowing out of the country in massive amounts, the participants were again asked to prepare a memorandum with the objectives of protecting the U.S. Cyberpayment industry from spillover damage caused by the Mexican Crisis. The participants were to recommend short term measures to respond to security problems in the systems and attempt to stimulate broader international measures to improve the industry.

STEP THREE. Return to the present/near future; lessons learned/ implications stage of the exercise. Participants were asked to address the challenge of formulating a strategy and policy "Action Plan" that would make thc hypothetical events portrayed in the foregoing scenario impossible, less likely, and/or more manageable.

Specific focus was placed on the development of ideas for: (1) government-industry cooperation and (2) regulatory, law enforcement, and legislative recommendations to prevent the potential abuse of Cyberpayment systems for money laundering.

A Hypothetical "Cyberpayment Network Targeting Order"

The exercise used a hypothetical analogue to a law enforcement technique used currently, the Geographic Targeting Order (GTO). A GTO gives the Treasury Department the authority to require a financial institution or a group of financial institutions in a geographic area to file special reports or maintain records beyond the ordinary requirements imposed by BSA regulations.

A recent GTO in New York in 1996-97 required 3,200 money transmitter agents to report identifying information on all cash remittances of $750 or more to Colombia. This led to a dramatic reduction in the volume of suspected drug-related funds flowing through money transmitters to Colombia, and triggered a number of large seizures of cash at air and sea ports along the eastern seaboard as traffickers shifted to more vulnerable means of moving their money.

The physical movement of cash remains a critical weak point in drug trafficker attempts to launder illicit funds. Therefore, GTOs are especially effective because of their ability to target a particular area of cash movement. The RAND exercise employed a hypothetical Cyberpayment Network Targeting Order (CNTO). The CNTO enabled law enforcement authorities to trace transfers of value within Cyberpayment networks. A combination of traditional investigative methods and the hypothetical CNTO was seen by some as a means of more effective detection of illicit activity within cyberspace. Others, however, saw it as beyond the bounds of existing law and technology.

The exercise illuminated potential problems flowing from the possible use of Cyberpayment systems by money launderers working for international narcotics cartels. Participants in the exercise discussed law enforcement and Cyberpayment oversight problems that flowed from the perceived abuse of these systems and evaluated potential remedial measures, such as the CNTO, for safeguarding Cyberpayment network security.

POTENTIAL POLICY IMPLICATIONS

Five general policy issues were identified in the exercise as areas of money laundering-related concern: (1) law enforcement issues; (2) regulatory issues; (3) international policy coordination; (4) Cyberpayment system architecture and design issues; and (5) traditional definitions of currency. Each of these issue areas carries important implications for the future of government and industry roles in managing these new payment system technologies so as to prevent their abuse. Because the exercise participants represented the entire spectrum of interests in this evolving technology, the responses to the exercises varied dramatically.

Participants considered these hypothetical policy issues within a decision-making process linked to the events of the scenario. Their responses were collected by exercise designers and reported to all participants during a discussion session led by the group chairpersons. This information was in turn analyzed by using the participants' annotated briefing books which contained individual responses to the questions presented during the exercises and operational notes taken by conference designers during exercise deliberations.

While no clear consensus on any overall approach to the potential concerns in the Cyberpayment-money laundering nexus was identified during the exercise, an important structuring and focusing of the debate in the five areas did occur. The findings listed below reflect RAND's evaluation of the focused discussion of the participants as well as RAND's independent research.

Due to the breadth of the subject, other larger issues concerning monetary policy and regulatory oversight emerged that were outside the direct scope of the exercise. Additional consideration of these issues, over time, will be needed to evaluate Cyberpayment systems and to ensure an effective and consistent process for governmental oversight.

Law Enforcement

The discussion of law enforcement issues focused predominantly on the perceived potential value of Cyberpayment instruments to money launderers and others attempting to conceal financial activities from government oversight. The second focus of these deliberations was on potential regulatory and law enforcement responses to perceived Cyberpayments abuse, and the place of computer-based investigative techniques alongside more traditional investigative techniques, in countering patterns of abuse.

Without proper precautions, Cyberpayment systems could have the potential to undermine traditional law enforcement investigative tools and techniques. Current anti-money laundering law enforcement strategies and techniques rely on extensive use of manpower and paper trails left by traditional monetary transactions. Since Cyberpayments are not personnel-intensive and could potentially leave little or no paper trail, they could facilitate a means for circumventing current techniques.

Law enforcement authorities may require new tools and techniques in order to conduct effective surveillance and analysis of Cyberpayment network information flows. Some international sharing of these information resources may also be required.

Computer-based investigative techniques may allow Cyberpayment system regulators and law enforcement authorities to trace questionable electronic fund flows. Law enforcement authorities may employ computer investigative techniques to evaluate information regarding suspected Cyberpayment system abuse. This evaluation depends, however, on some sort of infrastructure being developed for identifying value flows within networks that meet certain suspicious criteria, or more pointedly on differentiating Cyberpayment value from broader traffic flows within the Internet. International information sharing in pursuit of coordinated Cyberpayment system oversight and protection may involve risk. Jurisdictional issues involving federal, state, and local government law enforcement activities pertaining to potential Cyberpayment system abuse will need to be addressed if effective counters to potential abuse are to be implemented.

Individual privacy concerns are a significant issue in the design of oversight procedures for Cyberpayment systems. As noted, government concerns with the potential abuse of Cyberpayment systems create calls from some for extensive surveillance capabilities to be developed for Cyberpayment networks. However, this suggestion raises privacy concerns for individuals and potential constitutional issues for society. Consumer privacy advocates, in particular, have warned of possible abuses of surveillance techniques. Reconciling divergent perspectives on this issue will likely require continuous dialogue between and among the many stakeholders in the Cyberpayments arena.

Regulatory Issues

During the exercise, regulatory questions were perhaps the most vigorously discussed of any of the defining concerns involved with Cyberpayment systems. As an overlapping area of interest, regulatory concerns are themselves dependent on more general decisions on the importance of international policy coordination on the oversight of Cyberpayment systems, and on decisions regarding the legal character of Cyberpayment value as a payment instrument. Beginning with the issue of which institutions or entities would have the legal authority to provide Cyberpayment services, participants voiced a number of differing perspectives on the topic. A majority of participants argued that whichever regulatory approach was adopted, it should be based on the ongoing collaborative public-private partnership. Under this rubric, however, differences of opinion were voiced on the character and intrusiveness of governmental *mandates* with respect to both Cyberpayment system operators and the electronic payment instruments themselves.

Public-private collaboration will be key to crafting and implementing a coherent and sustainable Cyberpayment system infrastructure protection process. The expanding dialogue between government and private industry on Cyberpayment network standards and product features in the U.S. and elsewhere is a major positive step towards coming to grips with potential abuses of Cyberpayment systems. Many participants voiced concern that, at least initially, cyberpayment system providers that operate with or through banks should be subject to laundering controls analogous to those that apply to banks and other financial institutions.

Policy, regulation, and enforcement in the Cyberpayment area will consistently be challenged to keep up with the rapidly evolving technology. For the foreseeable future, law enforcement and financial payment system regulators will not experience a stable technical environment in the Cyberpayment arena. National regulations imposed in the absence of mature international technical and market standards will need to be inherently flexible in responding to this evolutionary environment. This situation could also inhibit the development of reliable technical means for tracing transactions within Cyberpayment networks when investigating illicit financial activity. One suggestion for addressing this concern was developing minimum standards for appropriate government access to Cyberpayment data as a condition of licensing – without prejudice to the particular encryption and product protection technologies implemented in a particular application.

Domestically, the U.S. government may need to play a facilitating role for both industry and consumers to accelerate the achievement of effective standards for Cyberpayment systems. Because of the centrality of financial payment systems to the U.S. economy and the potential impact of a commercially mature and successful Cyberpayment industry on our economy, a Cyberpayment system failure could negatively affect the credibility of the entire Cyberpayment industry. It was also suggested that the public perception that these systems are more (or less) prone to fraud or financial abuse than traditional payment methods may significantly affect consumer acceptance of Cyberpayment transactions. Any regulatory and law enforcement actions designed to monitor consumer behavior within the Cyberpayment environment will need to be closely integrated into a broader infrastructure assurance policy in order to protect the industry's acceptance in the financial marketplace.

International Policy Coordination

The discussion on international policy issues raised by the Cyberpayment systems focused on the degree to which national guidelines and regulations on system characteristics could be rendered ineffective and/or circumvented by international variation in oversight and regulations. Participants agreed that Cyberpayment products were inherently international in nature, and that any longer-term governmental actions would need to be international in scope.

International strategy and policy coordination will be central to effective Cyberpayment system oversight. The global nature of the Cyberpayment infrastructure suggests that some harmonization of guidelines and standards for Cyberpayment system operators will be imperative for effective oversight of the Cyberpayment industry. Because the Cyberpayment industry is evolving, a comprehensive and thorough regulatory regime is unlikely to be achieved prior to the stabilization of commercial and technical conditions. The recent discussions within a number of relatively recently established international bodies such as the G-7 Financial Action Task Force (FATF) have been an especially effective means for sharing insights on international Cyberpayment system oversight.

Cyberpayment System Architecture and Design

The discussion of Cyberpayment systems examined the question of whether this type of payment instrument posed potential impediments to law enforcement and payment system regulators in their investigation and enforcement of money laundering activity or whether particular types of Cyberpayment products constituted unique risks of abuse. Participants did not articulate a consensus on these issues, other than to observe that for security reasons, Cyberpayment system operators would tend to invest heavily in designing systems that minimized their degree of exposure to fraudulent use. These same measures could also be used against money laundering.

Both industry and government share an interest in developing technical and system standards that adequately reduce the possibility of fraud and financial crime. This observation was interpreted to mean that governments should attempt to achieve traditional oversight goals in the Cyberpayment area through voluntary compliance rather than through mandates.

The output from government/industry efforts to evaluate Cyberspace risks in key national infrastructures such as telecommunications, electric power and transportation need to be fed into the policy process for determining necessary actions for Cyberpayment infrastructure protection from money laundering. The President's Information Infrastructure Task Force recently stated that the Administration has already taken steps that will foster trust in encryption and provide safeguards that society will need. It also stated that it was working with Congress to enact legislation to facilitate development of voluntary management infrastructures that would govern the release of information to law enforcement officials pursuant to lawful authority.

Definitional Issues

Any interim definition of Cyberpayment value as possessing legal characteristics similar or equivalent to traditional paper currency (i.e., cash) will have to be monitored and perhaps adjusted due to frequent changes in the design of Cyberpayment products by industry. The issue of how Cyberpayment's value is to be defined, e.g., as cash, as funds transfers, monetary instruments or a new term, centered on establishing an appropriate regulatory oversight regime for Cyberpayment systems, while at the same time not imposing onerous (and costly) requirements on an evolving industry. It was generally felt that regulatory decisions should be made with an eye to not disadvantaging (or advantaging) any particular Cyberpayment system type, but rather that the marketplace should be allowed to make such determination.

RAND'S ANALYSIS

Three Models of Cyberpayment Oversight

The exercise deliberations yielded a number of differing viewpoints concerning the potential issues and opportunities created by the deployment of Cyberpayment systems. Participants offered perspectives on the role of government in Cyberpayment system oversight, the potential for industry self-regulation, and the difficulties of designing regulatory guidelines for a brand new industry.

RAND's analysis of participant deliberations has been categorized into three broad schools, or models, of potential Cyberpayment System Oversight. While a consensus on any one of the approaches was lacking, debate returned again and again to some general themes. The models, described below, are not mutually exclusive, but are related to one another. Combinations of these approaches will most likely eventually become the focus of the actual decision making on the appropriate oversight regime for Cyberpayment systems. It is important to point out, however, that controversies over whether government or industry are best suited to regulate this evolving industry are not ended by the adoption of any particular perspective on Cyberpayment system regulation. The *process* through which these issues are to be resolved may in fact be of greater importance than the particular end-point argued by proponents of any of the models in question.

Listed below each model are candidate plans that could be considered for that model in an attempt to shape constructively the emerging Cyberpayment system environment. Consistent with the debate among exercise participants, the plans and the models do not represent mutually exclusive approaches. The different perspectives are linked by critical assumptions such as the timing of Cyberpayment system deployments by private industry, and on the pace and character of consumer acceptance of the new payment instruments.

Model 1: Government Lead. Cyberpayment oversight could include a strong role for government in directing industry responses to potential Cyberpayment system vulnerabilities. This approach to oversight would anticipate only a few highly structured occasions where industry would be allowed to react to prospective rules.

Model 1 Candidate Plan

I. Issue an administrative finding that Cyberpayment value is to be treated as a cash equivalent for the purposes of anti-money laundering oversight.

II. Identify key Cyberpayment system features and begin a regulation writing process designed to bring these payment instruments into close scrutiny. Regulations drafted during this process would include:

- A definition of Cyberpayment instrument functionality including: denomination limits, peer-to-peer value transfer capabilities, system interoperability, and transaction frequency;
- Rules on the permissible issuers of Cyberpayment value;
- Mandates on the technologies contained in Cyberpayment instruments; and
- Mandates on system-audit and remote system management (under legal supervision) capabilities.

III. Initiate preparation of an international meeting involving senior finance ministry officials with a view to creating an international convention on the operation of Cyberpayment systems. Preparatory work would seek to establish common regulatory treatment of Cyberpayment issuers in all participating countries; to work out procedures to ensure the ability of states to enforce legal orders against Cyberpayment issuers or instrument holders whatever their country of residence; and to coordinate law enforcement action against international crime groups;

IV. The Administration would propose legislation, when necessary, establishing federal primacy in the oversight of Cyberpayment systems, and establishing tampering with Cyberpayment instruments (network or card-based) as a federal crime analogous to counterfeiting.

Model 2: Collaborative. This model emphasizes a more collaborative public-private sector partnership in Cyberpayment system oversight. This model envisions expanded governmental consultations with Cyberpayment system operators as the basis for regulatory action. Technical standards within Cyberpayment products would be decided by industry with government mandates only existing for systems used by government agencies to deliver services. Under this model, an independent government agency would administer a fixed set of rules governing the industry.

Model 2 Candidate Plan

I. Continue incremental regulatory action on Cyberpayment systems consistent with the pace of their introduction;

II. Begin a structured six-month set of consultations with industry designed to elicit input for a draft policy paper on Cyberpayment system oversight. The paper would address technology, regulatory, and law enforcement issues in both domestic and international dimensions. This paper would also support the U.S. negotiating position at the proposed meeting to establish an international convention on Cyberpayments system oversight. Industry and government officials would be equally represented in a steering committee through which the policy paper would be drafted.

III. Initiate experts meetings within the G-7 FATF or other international groups to discuss a short-list of the most pressing money laundering concerns of Cyberpayment systems from the points of view of payment system regulators and law enforcement authorities. These meetings would support a major international conference two years hence, at which senior finance ministry officials would be asked to draft a statement on the international oversight of Cyberpayment systems.

IV. Consult Cyberpayment industry representatives on the technical features necessary to establish CNTO-like system interrogation capabilities within planned Cyberpayment networks. Begin a regulation writing process in consultation with privacy advocates to mandate such capabilities for Cyberpayment systems if contacts with industry do not yield desired results.

V. Begin consultations where necessary with the U.S. Congress on the drafting of legal guidelines for law enforcement access to Cyberpayment records. In the interim, establish administrative guidelines for the use of these records by law enforcement authorities in criminal investigations.

Model 3: Self-Regulatory. Industry would be charged with setting and enforcing its own anti-money laundering standards under this regime, with government authorized to oversee this activity to ensure effective compliance. International oversight of Cyberpayment systems would take place on a government-to-government basis, but with industry enjoying key representation in governmental bodies charged with setting overall controls and oversight.

Model 3 Candidate Plan

I. Initiate a series of consultations with Cyberpayment industry representatives with a view to encouraging the establishment of an industry-wide association to represent commercial concerns in policymaking.

II. Seek legislation assigning functional responsibility for Cyberpayment systems to an established agency or new administrative body. A board made up equally of industry and government representatives would coordinate regulations in this functional area.

III. The Cyberpayment industry would be asked to provide – on demand – Cyberpayment records for government as needed during criminal investigations. This information access would be governed by administrative guidelines set up by the independent Cyberpayment oversight body, and would not be subject to judicial review.

It appeared that Model 1 conflicted the most with the contemporary trend which favors allowing the market to develop more fully before a regulatory scheme is adopted. Model 2 could be interpreted as a transitional stage, where models of industry-government collaboration could provide a "proof of principle" for concepts of industry self-regulation and governmental "arms length" supervision. This interpretation would leave Model 3 as an oversight framework perhaps best-suited when the market has matured. With established frameworks of industry-government and inter-governmental information and knowledge sharing, it is possible that this sort of oversight model could allow for the reconciliation of market efficiency and competitiveness concerns with public issues regarding financial privacy and the safety and soundness of the Cyberpayment industry.

The material that follows looks at the common action elements that might be included in a preparatory phase to any government oversight approach.

Common Elements

The introduction of Cyberpayment systems raise: (1) law enforcement issues; (2) regulatory issues; (3) need for international policy coordination; (4) Cyberpayment system architecture and design issues; and (5) non-traditional forms of payment with currency attributes. Work in any area would necessitate essentially *preparatory activity* for any more overarching regulatory project aimed at influencing Cyberpayment industry trends to reduce any money laundering vulnerabilities. A common preparatory phase of government action to guard against illicit uses of those systems could include:

- Conducting a baseline analysis of the technologies being used in proposed Cyberpayment system designs. This analysis would address: (1) the potential vulnerability of proposed technologies to "hacker" attack; (2) the ability of the system to deliver information on Cyberpayment value transfers to auditors; (3) the privacy implications of different Cyberpayment system architectures.

- Asking banks and non-banks (see Glossary) interested in operating Cyberpayment systems to respond to a list of security and abuse concerns generated by law enforcement and payment system regulators. (For the purpose of this report, non-banks will be identified as money services businesses (MSBs).) Required responses would address the critical information access concerns of the government in anticipation of broad deployment of Cyberpayment systems, and to react to scenario-based insights regarding potential patterns of abuse by criminals.

- Collecting and analyzing the results of the Cyberpayment industry submissions prior to the release of a preliminary policy paper by the U.S. Government (agency or agencies to be decided) that would constitute an initial government statement of regulatory preferences on Cyberpayment systems.

- Calling a special meeting of the FATF or some other international group, in order to begin structured experts meetings to discuss the technical standards and law enforcement issues raised by the emergence of Cyberpayment systems. This activity would be designed to coordinate with the U.S.-initiated Cyberpayment issuer requirement for response listed above.

- Convening a major conference involving senior Cyberpayment industry representatives, senior staff from the law enforcement community and potential payment system regulatory agencies, and international observers from international financial institutions as a final activity prior to the initiation of a formally introduced Cyberpayment anti-money laundering oversight policy. The objective of such a conference would be to achieve a degree of consensus on the character of emerging Cyberpayment systems, a consciousness of common regulatory and law enforcement challenges, and – where possible – agreement on the elements of a strategy for conducting such international oversight of Cyberpayment systems.

Candidate plans for addressing the potential money laundering problems posed by Cyberpayment systems share many common features. The principle differences among the plans are in the level of government mandates imposed upon Cyberpayment system operators. In turn, the scope of administrative action also varies, with the Models 1 and 2 seeking a binding international convention on Cyberpayment system oversight, and Model 3 initiating an industry-centered approach whose international version would likely include the largest private global financial institutions managing the sector on behalf of governments.

Combinations of these approaches, rather than any one perspective, are the most likely outcomes given the necessity for consensus-based action. Participants within the exercise considered the merits of government and industry-led actions to counter perceived Cyberpayment system vulnerabilities. While no clear consensus emerged, the predominant perspective in the deliberations supported close industry-government collaboration to address potential problems.

PREPARATION FOR ACTION

Participants in the exercise, whatever their particular positions on the action to be taken, did broadly share the idea that government needed to begin thinking of the appropriate regulatory and law enforcement actions necessary to adapt effectively to emerging Cyberpayment systems. Because new technologies are currently under pilot testing, government already confronts the potential need to include Cyberpayment system operators under some regulatory regime. This inclusion might be achieved in part through the creative extension of current anti money laundering requirements of banks and money service businesses to those seeking to deploy Cyberpayment products.

Analysis of the technologies and features of the new electronic payment systems is the first step toward understanding their implications for traditional anti-money laundering oversight rules. The entities most aware of the fast-changing technical state of the art are -- not surprisingly -- the commercial firms designing Cyberpayment products. Consequently, it is advisable that governments expand the dialogue with the private sector on the character of Cyberpayment products, including the security-related technical details intended to protect the financial integrity of Cyberpayment systems. Information gained during this process could contribute to a thoroughgoing evaluation of the appropriate policy environment for Cyberpayment products.

A BOTTOM LINE

What overall conclusions can be drawn from RAND's analysis of Cyberpayment systems and money laundering? The exercise experience revealed a wide scope of issues facing potential payment system regulators and the law enforcement community.

Prompt collaborative action by industry and government and among governments to prevent the exploitation of Cyberpayment system vulnerabilities is a critical way to respond to this still-nascent threat of exploitation by money launderers. Collaboration on standards, regulatory transparency, and vigorous surveillance of possible vulnerability exploitation offers the key to successful protection of Cyberpayment systems from such abuse. Furthermore, the scope of the potential money laundering problem is international. Effective law enforcement will require national governments to collaborate in setting the ground rules for Cyberpayment systems' deployment and operation.

The exercise provided a valuable arena in which policy and law enforcement issues raised by Cyberpayment systems could be examined. In the future, an extension of the simulation to include international participants would allow for a deeper understanding of the challenges involved. In turn, the exercise highlighted the importance of a harmonization of approaches to Cyberpayment system oversight to guard against and detect the illicit use of these systems. The danger that criminals will seek to exploit weaknesses in regulations wherever they appear suggests that governments need to coordinate investigative and enforcement activities aimed at minimizing this potential abuse.

While it is premature to draft a comprehensive oversight regime for Cyberpayment products, a structured dialogue involving government, issuing companies, and other stakeholders, will help to shape the direction of any such regime. The authors hope that the insights outlined in this report will assist in the advancement of public debate on Cyberpayment system security and the appropriate role for government in this rapidly growing segment of the Global Information Infrastructure.

ACKNOWLEDGMENTS

We are grateful for the contributions of many people within FinCEN, the Department of the Treasury, other government departments, within RAND, and industry to the conception and carrying out of this project. In particular, we would like to thank Shaun Lonergan and Thomas Firnhaber of FinCEN for contributions throughout the project. We would especially like to thank the staff of FinCEN who participated in the many tests of the exercise materials and those who helped to shape a report designed to clearly convey the results of this important effort.

We would especially like to express our appreciation to those who represented the following agencies at the May 5th and June 2nd exercise sessions:

Executive Office of the President
- Office of Science & Technology Policy
- Office of Management and Budget

Department of Justice
- Asset Forfeiture & Money Laundering Section
- Computer Crime & Intellectual Property Section
- U.S. Attorney's Office (Eastern District of NY)
- Federal Bureau of Investigation
- Drug Enforcement Administration

Department of Defense
- National Security Agency
- National Defense University
- U.S. Coast Guard Academy

Independent Agencies
- U.S. Department of State
- National Intelligence Council
- Sandia National Laboratory
- Federal Communications Commission
- Federal Trade Commission
- Securities and Exchange Commission
- Federal Deposit Insurance Corporation
- New York State Banking Department

Other
- National Association of Attorneys General
- Global Center of Leadership Trust
- Electronic Privacy Information Center
- Indiana University School of Law
- Georgetown University
- University of Kentucky School of Law
- National Security Research Inc.
- Fried, Frank, Harris, Shriver, & Jacobson
- Howrey & Simon

Department of Treasury
- Office of International Affairs
- Office of Intelligence Support
- Office of Financial Institutions Policy
- Office of Foreign Assets Control
- Financial Management Service
- U.S. Secret Service
- Bureau of Alcohol, Tobacco and Firearms
- Internal Revenue Service/Criminal Investigations Division
- U.S. Customs Service
- El Dorado Task Force
- Comptroller of the Currency
- Office of Thrift Supervision
- U.S. Mint

Federal Reserve
- Board of Governors of the Federal Reserve System
- Federal Reserve Bank of New York

U.S. Congress
- Senate Banking Committee
- Senate Select Committee on Intelligence
- Senate Appropriations Committee
- House Committee on Banking and Finance

Banking & Financial Industry
- American Bankers Association
- Consumers Bankers Association
- Citibank
- Chase Manhattan Bank
- Republic National Bank
- American Express
- Royal Bank of Canada
- Mondex International
- Mondex USA
- MasterCard International
- First Virtual Holdings Inc.
- Security First Network Bank, FSB
- Gemplus
- CyberCash Inc.
- GE Capital Services
- Western Union

1. INTRODUCTION

BACKGROUND

Cyberpayments are an emerging new class of instruments and payment systems that support the electronic transfer of value. These transfers may take place via networks, such as the Internet, or through the use of stored value-type smart cards. These new payment products are designed to replace cash for many retail and consumer-level transactions. Because of the efficiency and ease with which they transfer value, Cyberpayment systems also present new challenges to law enforcement. Technology exists which could permit these systems to combine the speed of the present bank-based wire transfer systems with the anonymity of currency. As a result, there are issues that must be addressed as these systems are being developed to ensure the prevention and detection of money laundering and other illegal financial transactions.

As portrayed in Figure 1.1, Cyberpayment systems essentially represent the product of the intersection between the ongoing revolution in information technology and a strong trend toward market deregulation that is carrying into the world of electronic commerce.

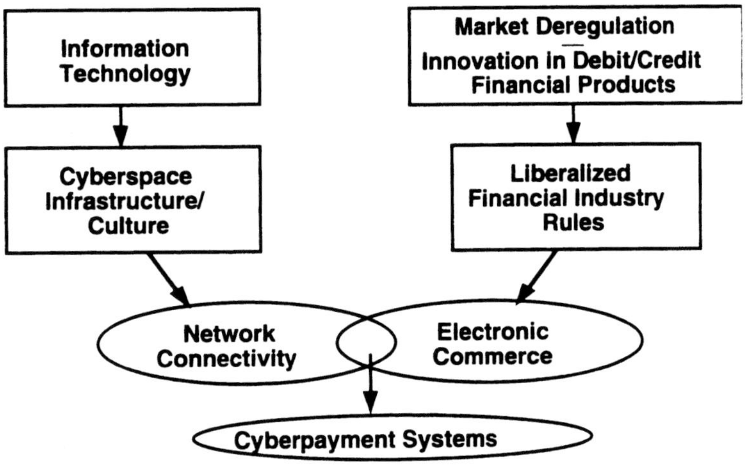

Figure 1.1. Cyberpayment Systems and Payment System Dynamics

The Financial Crimes Enforcement Network (FinCEN), an agency of the U.S. Department of the Treasury, sought RAND's assistance as part of an overall effort to examine potential money laundering concerns raised by the deployment of Cyberpayment systems. In furtherance of this general objective, FinCEN supports an extensive ongoing dialogue with the Cyberpayments industry.

FinCEN's first step in advancing this dialogue took place in September 1995, when it conducted a Cyberpayments Colloquium at the New York University School of Law. The Colloquium brought together financial services providers, software developers, academics, consumer representatives, and regulatory, policy, and law enforcement officials to discuss advances in the design and implementation of emerging electronic payment systems. In addition, in May 1996, FinCEN, in cooperation with the National Defense University, hosted a computer-based cyber-money laundering simulation exercise in which the participants used advanced decision making techniques to create hypothetical Cyberpayment-based money laundering scenarios.

Cyberpayment systems have also been a topic of interest to the White House, the United States Congress and various other law enforcement and regulatory agencies. In July 1997, the President released a report on the Global Information Infrastructure (GII), entitled "A Framework for Global Electronic Commerce," a portion of which directly addressed Cyberpayment issues. In addition, Cyberpayment systems were the subject of hearings conducted in 1996 by the Subcommittee on Domestic and International Monetary Policy of the House Banking and Financial Services Committee.

Internationally, Cyberpayment systems have also received extensive attention. Multilateral discussions and studies have been undertaken by both the G-7's Financial Action Task Force (FATF) and the G-10's Working Party On Electronic Money. In June 1996, a new recommendation #13 was added to the FATF's 40 Recommendations. It states that "[c]ountries should pay special attention to money laundering threats inherent in new or developing technologies that may favor anonymity, and take measures, if needed, to prevent their use in money laundering schemes."

MONEY LAUNDERING CONCERNS

Credit and debit cards allow their users to purchase goods and services without the use of cash, but invariably involve an intermediary financial institution or credit card issuer. In contrast, a central characteristic of many emerging Cyberpayment systems is the phenomenon of *disintermediation* -- the absence of a regulated third party (e.g., a bank) in transfers of financial value between two or more entities. The empowerment of individuals to transfer electronic cash equivalents across information networks without intermediation significantly lowers transactions costs. In effect, economic competitiveness and efficiency motivations are thus fostering the expansion of network connectivity to new user communities that demand new types of payment instruments that pose significant challenges for law enforcement authorities and payment system regulators.

The international dimension of these systems, and the fact that value transfers may take place with rapidity and with a degree of anonymity that impedes oversight by governmental authorities, is clearly a serious concern.

PURPOSE OF RAND RESEARCH EFFORT

The goal of this research effort is to explore the dimensions and implications of potential future illicit uses of Cyberpayment systems by money launderers and others seeking to conceal funds from governmental authorities. This research is also intended to identify -- at least in a preliminary fashion -- possible law enforcement and regulatory responses to potential patterns of Cyberpayment system misuse.

The application of new information technologies to Cyberpayment systems is still in its infancy. How these systems develop will depend on a combination of the effectiveness and efficiency of these technologies, the market, and consumer acceptance. However, many aspects of system design are likely to be decided in the next few years as Cyberpayments go through an "early adopter" phase of partial market exploitation. For reasons such as these, it is important for law enforcement and regulators to work more closely with Cyberpayment system developers to better understand the broad range of system design and other issues that are under consideration as markets and technologies mature.

Cyberpayment industry representatives for their part have stated that they both want and need more feedback from law enforcement in order to understand better anti-money laundering concerns. Clearly, only with such interaction can industry incorporate possible anti-money laundering solutions into their emerging systems.

In response to this situation, law enforcement must continue to improve its efforts to reach out to industry to better understand the commercial concerns of emerging Cyberpayment system operators. For example, measures that are necessary for anti-money laundering purposes should be considered alongside those safeguards that the industry is already building into its systems to prevent fraud and meet other security concerns.

The RAND research effort was designed to support these objectives.

THE RAND EXERCISE

To address FinCEN's interest in this emerging area, RAND designed, conducted, and analyzed a strategic decision-making exercise directed at both the potential problems and opportunities that the emergence of Cyberpayment systems pose for U.S. and global anti-money laundering efforts.

To accomplish the project's research goals, the exercise sought to achieve four primary tasks:

1. Describe current Cyberpayment concepts and systems.
2. Identify an initial set of Cyberpayment characteristics of particular concern to law enforcement and payment system regulators.
3. Identify major issues Cyberpayment policies will need to address.
4. Array appropriate approaches to address potential Cyberpayment system abuse in a set of potential action plans.

Participants in the exercise included a range of representatives from the Executive Branch, the Cyberpayment industry, the banking industry, the Congress, and academia. Responses to potential Cyberpayment misuse were compiled through recording the exercise experiences of participants, and through observation and analysis of dilemmas posed by the exercise itself. During this process, traditional law enforcement and regulatory measures were compared to the potentially new challenges posed by Cyberpayment technologies. The extensive participation of Cyberpayment industry representatives made it possible to gain a working knowledge of the rapidly evolving state of the art.

Because of the challenge of educating exercise participants about both Cyberpayments and money laundering, the exercise was built on a familiar scenario framework -- drug cartels and money laundering. The hypothesis was that drug cartels would become early adopters of Cyberpayments for money laundering. The time frame for the scenario was intended to be far enough into the future (2004) so that Cyberpayment systems would have progressed substantially, but not to the point where the market and technology for such systems had fully matured.

In support of this scenario, a "future history" was developed that described: (1) hypothetical developments in Cyberpayment systems; (2) the emergence of criminal exploitation of Cyberpayment systems for money laundering; (3) international and U.S. responses to this challenge; and (4) hypothetical drug cartel exploitation of Mexican Cyberpayment systems for money laundering in the context of a Mexican drug war.

ORGANIZATION OF THE REPORT

The remaining chapters of this report are organized as follows. Chapter Two provides a primer on criminal money-laundering processes. Chapter Three describes the range of emerging Cyberpayment technologies. Chapter Four describes potential abuses of Cyberpayment Systems for money laundering and other illegal transactions and the challenge these techniques pose for law enforcement. Chapter Five presents findings from the exercise. Chapter Six presents conclusions. The Appendices present the methodology employed in the exercise in greater detail and the exercise materials.

2. MONEY LAUNDERING

TRADITIONAL MONEY LAUNDERING PROCESSES

Money laundering is an illegal activity through which criminal proceeds take on the outward appearance of legitimacy. It is an integral support function common to virtually all profit-producing criminal activities. The U.S. Criminal Code contains more than 100 predicate offenses to the crime of money laundering. These offenses, referred to as "specified unlawful activities," range from narcotics trafficking and financial fraud, to kidnapping and espionage.

In most financial transactions, there is a financial trail to link the funds to the person(s) involved. Criminals avoid using traditional payment systems, such as checks, credit cards, etc., because of this paper trail. They prefer to use cash because it is anonymous. Physical cash, however, has disadvantages. It is bulky and difficult to move. For example, 44 pounds of cocaine worth $1 million equals 256 pounds of street cash worth $1 million. The street cash is more than six times the weight of the drugs. The existing payment systems and cash are both problems for criminals. Even more so for large transnational organized crime groups. Regulations and banking controls have increased costs and risks.

The physical movement of large quantities of cash is the money launderer's biggest problem. To better understand the potential for abuse of Cyberpayment systems to launder money, a brief explanation of how criminals "legitimize" cash through the traditional money laundering process is provided.

Placement, *layering* and *integration* are terms used by law enforcement to describe the three stages through which criminal proceeds are laundered.

Placement. Placement is the first stage in the money laundering process. It is during the placement stage that physical currency enters the financial system and illegal proceeds are most vulnerable to detection. When illicit monies are deposited at a financial institution, placement has occurred. The purchase of money orders using cash from a criminal enterprise is another example of placement. The Bank Secrecy Act (BSA) (see Table 2.1) and related regulations mandate the reporting of certain types of financial transactions which involve cash and/or certain monetary instruments. To conceal their activities money launderers must either circumvent the legitimate financial system entirely, or violate reporting/record-keeping rules established under the BSA. Accordingly, law enforcement officials, working in cooperation with the financial industry, are in a unique position to combat money laundering during this stage.

Layering. Layering describes an activity intended to obscure the trail which is left by "dirty" money. During the layering stage, a launderer may conduct a series of financial transactions in order to build layers between the funds and their illicit source. For example, a series of bank-to-bank funds transfers would constitute layering. Activities of this nature, particularly when they involve funds transfers between tax haven and bank secrecy jurisdictions, can make it very difficult for investigators to follow the trail of money.

Integration. During the final stage in the laundering process, illicit funds are integrated with monies from legitimate commercial activities as they enter the mainstream economy. The illicit funds thus take on the appearance of legitimacy. The integration of illicit monies into a legitimate economy is very difficult to detect unless an audit trail had been established during the placement or layering stages.

TABLE 2.1

The Bank Secrecy Act

The Bank Secrecy Act (BSA), authorizes the Secretary of the Treasury to issue regulations requiring financial institutions to keep certain records and file certain reports, and to implement anti-money laundering programs and compliance procedures. For the purposes of the BSA, "financial institution" is defined broadly to include, inter alia, a bank, a broker or dealer in securities, a currency dealer or exchanger, or a casino.

The BSA was enacted in 1970 in response to concern over the use of financial institutions by criminals to disguise the proceeds of their illicit activity. The purpose of the BSA and its implementing regulations is to provide law enforcement authorities with the tools necessary to combat these problems by "requiring certain reports or records where they have a high degree of usefulness in criminal, tax, or regulatory investigations or proceedings." Reports required under the BSA include: suspicious activity reports, currency transaction reports, reports of cross-border movements of currency and monetary instruments, and reports on foreign bank accounts. Two of these BSA reports are described below:

Currency Transaction Report (CTR): Covered financial institutions must file a CTR for each transaction in which they are involved that exceeds $10,000. Under this requirement, multiple currency transactions are treated as a single transaction if they total more than $10,000 during any one business day. The $10,000 reporting threshold may, in certain circumstances, be modified by the Secretary, (see discussion of Geographic Targeting Orders in Chapter 6)

Report of International Transportation of Currency and Monetary Instruments (CMIR): Each person must make a CMIR declaration when he or she physically transports currency or other monetary instruments in an aggregate exceeding $10,000 at one time, into or out of the United States.

Generally, a person willfully violating the BSA or its implementing regulations is subject to a criminal fine up to $250,000 or a five-year term of imprisonment, or both. A person who makes such a violation while violating another law of the United States, or engaging in a pattern of illegal activity, is subject to a criminal fine of up to $500,000 or a ten-year term of imprisonment, or both.

MONEY LAUNDERING SCHEMES

Money laundering schemes may vary greatly in character and complexity. They may involve any number of intermediaries and utilize both traditional and non-traditional payment systems. To a large extent, the scope and nature of a money laundering operation is limited only by the creativity of those involved. International narcotics traffickers may employ a variety of different money laundering techniques and schemes at any one time, each specially created to fulfill specific goals and objectives.

Advanced computing and communications technologies are currently routinely used to enhance the efficiency and the security of narcotics-related money laundering operations.

The examples which follow below are base-line schemes intended to familiarize the reader with a few simple methods for moving illicit funds.

Example #1 (Figure 2.1): Move U.S.-based funds to Mexico for use in local economy.

1. Street level narcotics sales occur in the U.S. (cash is the preferred method of payment for these transactions.)
2. The cash from one or multiple sales locations is collected at a safe or "stash" house for processing.
3. The cash is taken to a remittance business for transmission out of the country. To avoid scrutiny by law enforcement or bank regulatory authorities, the cash may be divided into amounts less than $10,000 and "smurfed" (the employment of a large number of individuals to make small deposits and withdrawals) or structured (transfer of amounts below federal reporting requirements) at the remittance business.
4. The funds are sent by the U.S.-based remitter to a Mexican-based counterpart. (The remittance company will normally utilize an offsetting book entry transfer or conduct a bank wire transfer in order to move the money out of the United States.)
5. The remittance business in Mexico pays out in Pesos.

Example #2 (Figure 2.2): Move Laundered Funds from U.S. to Mexico.

1. Money from U.S. drug sales is converted into money orders.
2. Money orders are shipped to Colombia via express mail.
3. U.S. funds money orders are sold to a currency broker in exchange for Pesos.

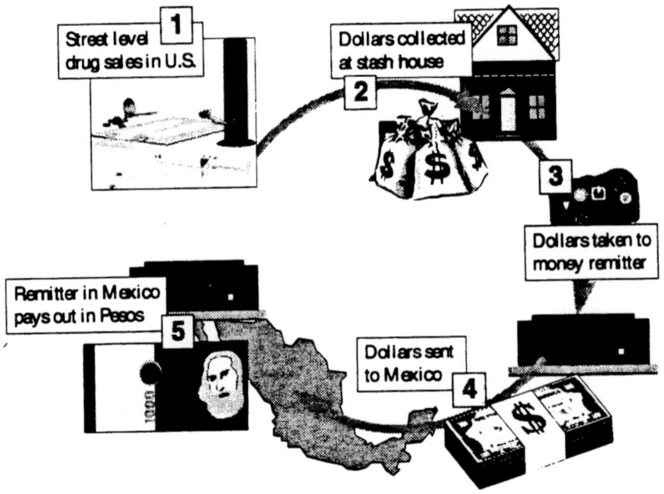

Figure 2.1. Movement of Funds from the U.S to Mexico

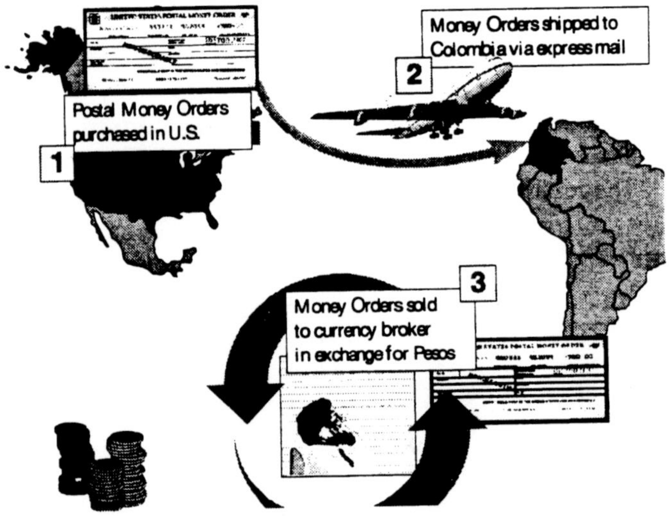

Figure 2.2. Move Laundered Funds from the U.S. to Mexico

GEOGRAPHIC TARGETING ORDERS AND ANTI-MONEY LAUNDERING POLICIES

The speed and "paperless" nature of Cyberpayment transactions pose potential challenges for traditional methods of policing illegal cash transactions. These methods of preventing, detecting, and combating money laundering are characterized by techniques that require large numbers of personnel. Extensive coordination of law enforcement activities among federal, state, and local police agencies is also critical to the effective implementation of anti-money-laundering initiatives.

A Geographic Targeting Order (GTO) is one technique used by law enforcement authorities to investigate money-laundering activities relating to drug trafficking. A GTO gives the Treasury Department the authority to require a financial institution or a group of financial institutions in a geographic area to file additional reports or maintain additional records above and beyond the ordinary requirements imposed by BSA regulations.

A GTO initiated in New York in 1996 (and extended into 1997) required at one point, 23 money transmitters and their approximately 3200 agents to report identifying information on all cash remittances of $750 or more to Colombia. This led to a dramatic reduction in the volume of suspected drug related funds flowing through money transmitters to Colombia, and triggered a number of large seizures of cash at air and sea ports along the eastern seaboard as traffickers shifted to more vulnerable means of moving their money.

A GTO thus has at least two important and complementary functions. First, it serves as an information gathering device that enables law enforcement authorities to gain greater knowledge of patterns of money laundering. The information gathered helps to establish better estimates of the volume of illicit funds laundered, and assists in more effective targeting of illegal activities by law enforcement. Second, a GTO helps to prevent evasion of the BSA regulations by disturbing established patterns of money laundering through the introduction of uncertainty and heightened risk into the cost-benefit and other calculations of drug traffickers and others who would circumvent the standard BSA reporting and record keeping requirements. This preventive function is a significant part of the value of GTOs to law enforcement's anti-money laundering efforts.

The physical movement of cash remains a critical weak point in drug trafficker attempts to launder illicit funds. Targeting particularly vulnerable industries or industry segments -- such as money transmitters sending funds to Colombia -- increases the transparency of a particular type of financial transaction while also creating a "money disposal" problem for drug traffickers. This implicit rise in the "price" of handling cash derived from illegal activities is a key variable in the "economics" of the drug business. In this sense, price shifts in the cost of money laundering may cause money launderers to seek alternative ways to move their funds into the legitimate financial systems.

GTOS AND NEW PAYMENT SYSTEM TECHNOLOGIES

GTOs have been implemented four times -- in Phoenix in 1989, in Houston in 1991, in New York from August 1996 to October 1997, with respect to cash purchased remittances to Colombia, and in New York and Puerto Rico from September 1997 to the present with respect to cash purchased remittances to the Dominican Republic. The success of the Colombia operation is attributable in large part to the commitment of considerable resources and personnel to its planning, implementation and follow-up. Even if resource limits *did not* restrict the use of these methods, their long-term utility could be affected by the emergence of Cyberpayment system technologies.

Law enforcement techniques may need to adapt very rapidly to these emerging technical possibilities while at same time seeking to maximize the effectiveness of existing investigative techniques. The development of new law enforcement investigative techniques is a necessary complement to the continuing utility of traditional investigative methods. Consistent with concerns for minimizing the cost of oversight requirements on Cyberpayment system operators, proposed governmental regulations were evaluated by industry participants during the exercise process. In addition, Cyberpayment industry representatives were consulted throughout the exercise design process with a view to assessing the technical feasibility of proposed investigative techniques against the known (though dynamic) characteristics of deploying Cyberpayment systems.

3. CYBERPAYMENT SYSTEMS

OVERVIEW

There is a broad range of Cyberpayment systems currently under development. Two dominant generic types of systems currently in development, testing, and (in a few cases) operation are extensively cited and employed in the exercise: (1) Stored value smart cards, and (2) Internet-based payment systems (e.g., electronic cash" or "e-cash"). Recent developments indicate that these two technologies are in the process of converging, which could create a unified Cyberpayment infrastructure containing a variety of payment products.

Progress towards technical and commercial standards in the Cyberpayments industry has been steady. However, financial interoperability -- clearing and settlement, and associated financial liability issues between issuing institutions in different countries -- may in some cases prove extremely difficult. This is likely to lead to system-level controls (as in the credit card industry) in an effort to discourage abuse in any particular country.

Cyberpayment systems are able to take advantage of the deployment of various network technologies by other entities such as telecommunications and computer companies. These companies have constructed and continue to plan the deployment of software and hardware systems to bring an ever larger number of ever more capable networks to new user communities.

Some Cyberpayment instrument features such as peer-to-peer value transfer and payer anonymity offer to the consumer an instrument with much of the flexibility and convenience of cash together with an enhanced ability to conduct purchases on an almost global basis. As a consequence government authorities may, at some point, confront an environment where Cyberpayment instruments substantially reduce the use of physical currency in consumer-level transactions.

In considering the Cyberpayments-money laundering nexus, it should be noted that the same technologies underlying Cyberpayment products could also be used as new information gathering tools by law enforcement and payment system regulators. The privacy implications of enhanced government surveillance of information networks is an issue that was addressed at considerable length during the exercise. Policies in this area must be carefully crafted so as to meet constitutional protections of individual privacy and governmental concerns with critical infrastructure protection.

FOUR MODELS OF CYBERPAYMENT SYSTEMS

Within this emerging and still evolving infrastructure, four basic examples of Cyberpayment systems are described below:

1. The Merchant Issuer Model (Figure 3.1). Smart card issuer and seller of goods are the same. Example: the Creative Star farecard used by riders of the Hong Kong transit system.

2. The Bank Issuer Model (Figure 3.2). Merchant and smart card issuer are different parties. Transactions are cleared through traditional financial systems. Examples: Banksys' Proton card in Belgium (now licensed by American Express) and the Danmont card in Denmark.
3. Non-Bank Issuer Model (Figure 3.3). Users buy electronic cash from issuers using traditional money and spend the electronic cash at participating merchants. Issuer subsequently redeems the electronic cash from the merchant. Example: CyberCash's electronic coin product.
4. Peer-to-Peer Model (Figure 3.4). Bank or non-bank issued electronic cash is transferable between users. Only point of contact between the traditional payments system and electronic cash is the initial purchase of electronic cash from the issuer and redemption of electronic cash from individuals or merchants. Example: Peer-to-Peer value transfers through the MONDEX stored value smart card.

The four models allow value to be added to or transferred from stored value-type smart cards using a variety of vehicles.

DEVELOPMENTS IN CYBERPAYMENT SYSTEMS

A number of Cyberpayment system pilots have been launched in different parts of the world. (In general, bank and credit card consortia have created joint ventures to test consumer acceptance of these new payment instruments.) Some believe that stored value-type smart cards and Internet-based payments products will develop and be accepted quickly creating a Cyberpayment infrastructure with varying characteristics and a number of different electronic payment products. Others believe, given the growing success of debit cards and other more conventional payment methods, that this process will be much more prolonged.

The material which follows describes examples of stored value smart card and Internet-based payment system initiatives.

One well-known pilot program is the MONDEX stored value smart card which is being tested in the U.K., Canada, the U.S., Hong Kong, New Zealand, and Australia. In November of 1996, MasterCard International purchased 51 per cent of MONDEX International; and in December of 1996 seven major US corporations joined together to establish MONDEX USA, a firm designed to commercially develop and implement the MONDEX electronic cash system in the US. Participating corporations in the MONDEX USA venture are: Wells Fargo, MasterCard, AT&T Universal card Services, Discover card, Michigan National Bank, Chase Manhattan Bank, and First Chicago. In September of 1996, MONDEX International signed a joint development agreement with CyberCash (an Internet-based payment system provider - see below) to integrate MONDEX's stored value smart card technology with CyberCash's electronic wallet.

American Express will use Proton Electronic Purse technology to implement multiple stored value smart card pilots over the next year. Proton (owned by BANKSYS) is already being either piloted or rolled out in Canada, Australia, Sweden, Belgium, Brazil, the Netherlands and Switzerland.

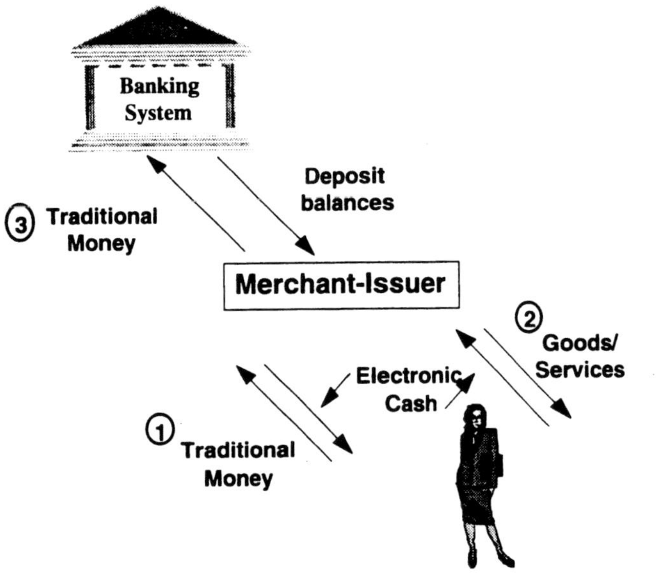

Figure 3.1. Merchant Issuer Model

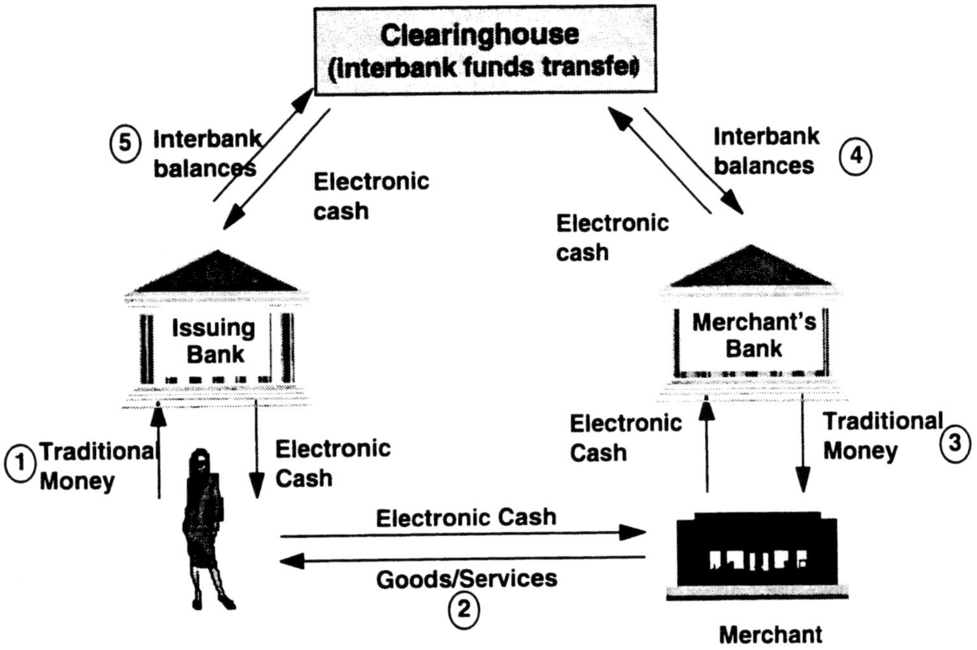

Figure 3.2. Bank Issuer Model

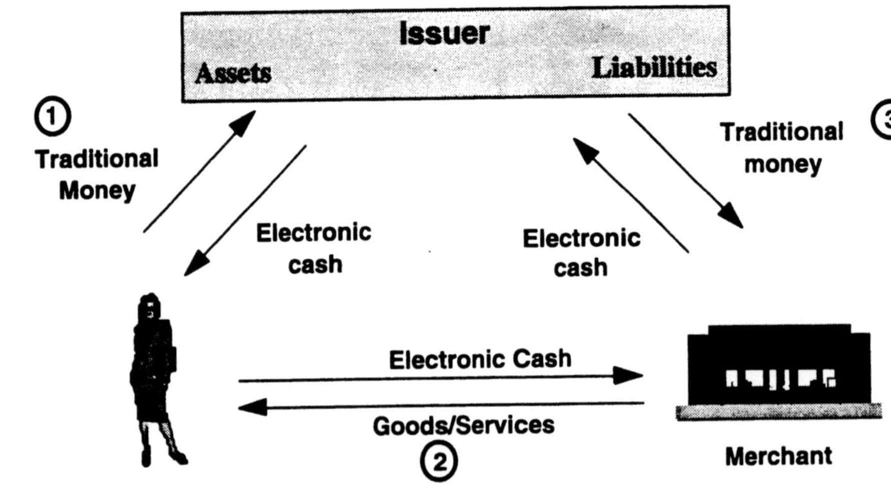

Figure 3.3. Non-Bank Issuer Model

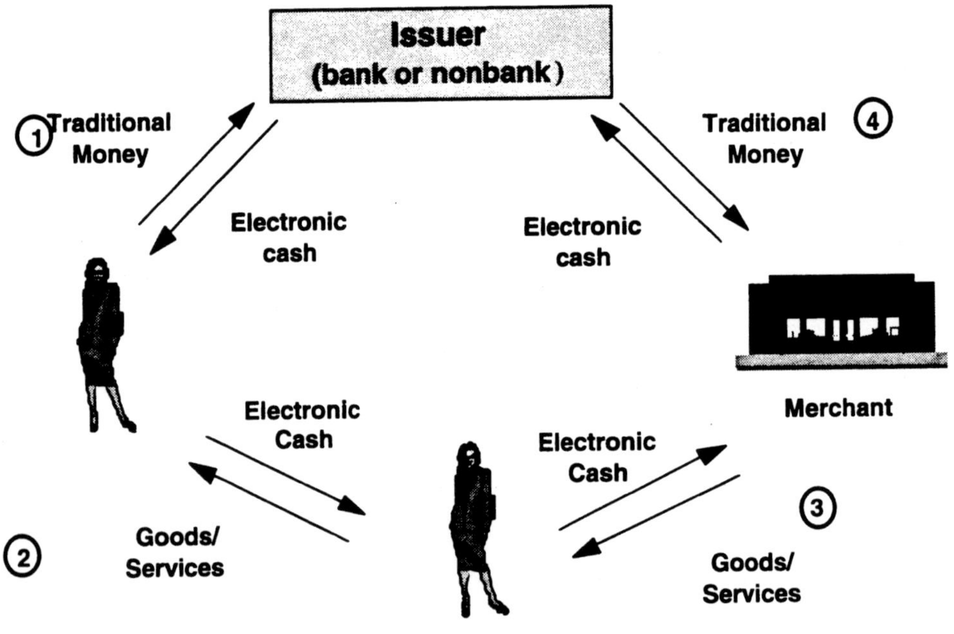

Figure 3.4. Peer-to-Peer Model

First Union, NationsBank, Wachovia, Citicorp and other banks around the world are piloting the VisaCash smart card. A VisaCash smart card product, is currently in a worldwide pilot test with launches in 1996 in Atlanta, Buenos Aires, Bogota, South Africa, Hong Kong and Australia and a test planned for 1997 in Manhattan. Other stored value smart card experiments have been launched in South Africa, Western Europe, Russia, Hong Kong, and China.

In the Internet-based payment systems arena two well-known companies are CyberCash and Digicash. Each of these companies has initiated joint venture agreements with participating financial institutions to ensure the compatibility of their products. In October of 1996, Netscape agreed to bundle CyberCash's electronic wallet with its browser and server software products. Later on in the year, Microsoft agreed to integrate CyberCash's electronic wallet technology into its new Internet commerce server production. Participants in the CyberCash payment system include MONDEX, America On Line, IBM, Microsoft, VISA and more than 40 other banks and financial service providers.

Participants in the Digicash payment system include Mark Twain Bank, (U.S.), Deutsche Bank (Germany), MERITA (Finland), and ADVANCE (Australia).

4. THE POTENTIAL EXPLOITATION OF CYBERPAYMENTS SYSTEMS FOR MONEY LAUNDERING

INTRODUCTION

The RAND exercise focused on identifying potential characteristics in Cyberpayment systems that could be exploited by money launderers. By their nature, Cyberpayment systems have the potential to eliminate the money launderer's biggest problem, the physical movement of large amounts of cash. The globalization of many proposed Cyberpayment systems may also offer money launderers opportunities to exploit national differences in security standards and oversight rules to conceal the movement of illicit funds.

Previous forums have identified a number of features that law enforcement must consider with respect to Cyberpayment transactions. Among them are (1) Disintermediation; (2) Bank or Non-Bank Issuance; (3) Peer-to-Peer Transfers; (4) Transaction Anonymity and; (5) Denomination Limits and Expiration Dates. Each of these basic features is described in more detail below. While these basic features make Cyberpayments attractive as a potential means to reduce transaction costs in commerce and contribute to the increased efficiency of the economy, these features are also consistent with vulnerabilities that may be exploited by criminals.

Disintermediation. Historically, law enforcement and regulatory officials have relied on the intermediation of banks and other regulated financial institutions to provide "choke points" through which funds must generally pass and where records would be maintained. Disintermediation involves the transfer of financial value between entities without the intermediate involvement of an identifiable third party subject to governmental oversight (e.g., record-keeping requirements via a bank). Should Cyberpayment systems permit disintermediated value transfers in unlimited amounts, money launderers could use this as an opportunity to avoid traditional law enforcement money tracing methods.

Bank and Non-Bank Issuance. Bank and non-bank entities may be subject to different rules regarding their operation of Cyberpayment systems. This difference is already the case in several nations where non-bank Cyberpayment issuers are currently subject to a different set of rules from banks. A simple extension of traditional payment system oversight to new non-bank Cyberpayment issuers may address some of the concerns regarding potential system abuse. However, the new systems are configured differently and constantly mutating, so a "one size fits all" regulatory approach is not necessarily appropriate or even possible.

Peer-To-Peer Transfers of Value. Some Cyberpayment systems allow consumers to transfer value peer-to-peer (and thus, disintermediated) using an electronic "wallet," a telephone, or via the Internet. Such value transfers pose perhaps the most direct challenge to governmental oversight of Cyberpayment systems. In the absence of intelligence information or evidence from non-Cyberpayment system sources (e.g., physical surveillance) triggering an investigation into specific suspect stored value instrument activity, peer-to-peer transfers of value are unlikely to be detected.

Transaction Anonymity. In some emerging Cyberpayment products, the origins of funds are relatively opaque and the identity of the individual or entity transferring them difficult to determine. In fact, payer anonymity (the identity of the party initiating a Cyberpayment value transfer) is a central characteristic of some proposed systems. For Cyberpayment value transfers (e.g., via the Internet or the basic telephone system), transaction anonymity could be an almost insuperable barrier to law enforcement detection. While candidate solutions for this problem have been put forward, they raise issues concerning individual privacy.

Denomination Limits and Expiration Dates. Cyberpayment product issuers are likely to limit the maximum amounts that can be stored on smart cards or other devices, to reduce the risks of fraud or other losses. As with credit cards, Cyberpayment issuers will also likely establish needs-based denomination limits that would be determined by commercial and market factors. (Recent consumer tests of Cyberpayment systems indicate likely consumer limits of approximately $1,000 - $3,000). Cyberpayment products held by retailers are likely to have a much larger value limit than those for most individuals and differ widely between retailers. Cyberpayment value could also be programmed to expire after a certain number of transfers. As early technology adopters, money launderers could be expected to exploit whatever limits are established, just as they do now by structuring transactions under currency reporting limits, obtaining multiple cards (credit or debit), using multiple names, or employing multiple issuers.

Table 4.1 illustrates the current or soon to be implemented methods of adding and transferring value and the potential availability of records associated with each. (As these systems mature, additional methods of adding and transferring value may be developed.) Table 4.1 suggests that the primary determinant of the availability, quantity, and quality of transaction records is the source of funds added to or transferred from the stored value card/electronic purse. The more an electronic payment system emulates currency, the greater the likelihood that transaction records will be limited. Note, however, that in some instances a limited number of the most recent transactions are recorded. For example, an individual's stored value card may contain a transaction log of the card's most recent 20 transactions, once the 21st transaction is conducted, the first one will be lost.

Table 4.1.

Comparison of Potential Transaction Records

Source of Funds	Loading/Transfer Vehicle	Record Type	Record Location
Cash	Kiosk	Possibly No Record	On Machine (?)
Customer's Checking or Savings Account	ATM, Personal Computer, Telephone (Pay or personal), or Cellular Phone	Record of transfer from customer's account. (Similar to cash withdrawal)	Card Issuing Institution
Retail Sales	Merchant Terminal at a traditional store and/or Internet Mall.	Transaction Log: card identifier & amount for a limited number of the most recent transaction are recorded.	Merchant's Electronic Wallet
Peer-to-Peer transfer of e-cash stored in a smart card or Electronic Wallet	Electronic Wallet, PC, Telephone or Cellular Phone	Transaction Log: card identifier & amount of a limited number of the most recent transactions are recorded.	Stored Value card or Electronic Wallet

USING CYBERPAYMENTS TO LAUNDER MONEY: HYPOTHETICAL EXAMPLES

Both variants of Cyberpayment instruments – network-based systems and stored value-type smart cards – offer particular opportunities for money launderers to conceal the movement of illicit funds. A few examples of the kinds of activities money launderers may attempt using Cyberpayment instruments help to make clear the potential for abuse within Cyberpayment networks.

The Street Drug Market

In this example (see Figure 4.1) drugs would be sold to users in exchange for disposable smart cards denominated in amounts typically associated with street drug transactions -- $20, $50, or even $100. These smart cards would be collected by the street drug dealer and taken to a retail store. The merchant would then upload the electronic value from the smart cards from his/her merchant terminal to a bank or funds-holding account at a financial institution.

The merchant would most likely receive a standard fee for the use of his/her value upload capabilities. Once the funds have entered the legitimate payment system, the funds could then be transferred to a domestic or offshore account in a process analogous to the placement, layering, and integration phases of traditional money laundering.

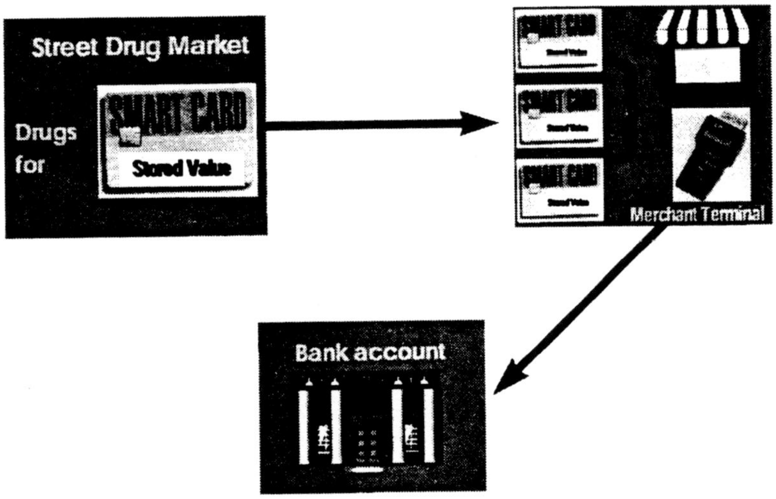

Figure 4.1. The Street Drug Market

Two Types of Cyberpayment Value Transfer

In this example (see Figure 4.2) stored value derived from drug-trafficking activity could be transferred in at least two simple ways. Perhaps the most predictable manner of funds movement is through the physical transport of high-value, stored value smart cards containing the proceeds of drug trafficking. Because of their small size these cards could be easily concealed and eventually disposed of through redeposit of the funds in a foreign country.

A second way of transporting/transferring value beyond the reach of law enforcement authorities could be to transfer stored value over smart card enabled telephones. Both cellular and conventional analog telephones are being designed to enable them to inter-operate with stored value smart cards. Such products could obviate the need to launder funds by offering criminals an impressively rapid and efficient means for transferring and consolidating a stream of illicit funds such as those derived from drug trafficking. Once funds enter the payment system they are indistinguishable from funds derived from legitimate sources.

Funds Transfers through Network-based Systems

In this example (see Figure 4.3) low denomination stored value smart cards could transfer their value onto personal computers which would then transfer that value over the Internet, using increasingly available anonymous remailers to conceal the points of origin of illicit funds. Recipients could then consolidate funds and reintegrate them into the payment system.

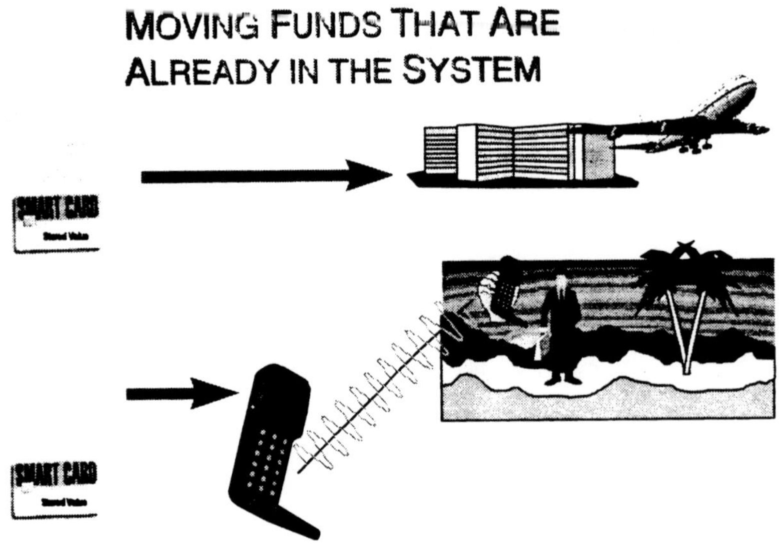

Figure 4.2. Two Types of Cyberpayment Value Transfer

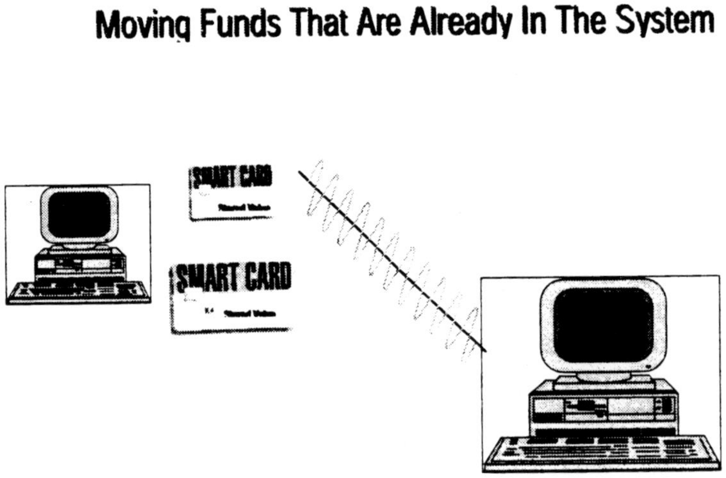

Figure 4.3. Funds Transfers Through Network-based Systems

Cyberpayment Value and the World Wide Web

The last example of Cyberpayment system misuse (see Figure 4.4) involves a fraudulent charity that only accepts electronic value (Cyberpayment value) as donations. Funds collected for an apparently legitimate charity could instead represent the proceeds of drug trafficking. These funds could be uploaded from the electronic purses on PCs to a bank account, and then redistributed from one financial institution to another individual or group elsewhere in the world.

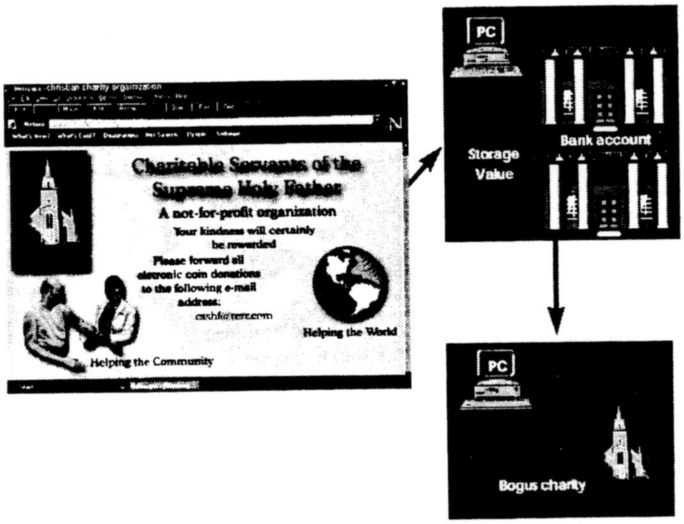

Figure 4.4. Cyberpayment Value Transfers over the World Wide Web

CYBERPAYMENT NETWORK-BASED INVESTIGATIVE TECHNIQUES

One proposal that emerged from the exercise for tracing value within Cyberpayment networks was a cyberspace analog to the GTO -- a Cyberpayment Network Targeting Order (CNTO). A combination of traditional and non-traditional investigative means, this hypothetical new investigative technique was seen as a potential means of more effective detection of illicit activity within cyberspace, and thus more efficient allocation of limited law enforcement resources.

The CNTO Concept

The CNTO concept is a hypothetical construct that was developed for the purposes of the exercise component of this research project. In the exercise it was assumed that: (1) like the GTO, the authority to implement an CNTO is already within the Bank Secrecy Act (with the CNTO concept approved on this basis) and (2) the concept functions effectively in real-world Cyberpayment environments.

The essence of the CNTO tool is the exploitation - with proper legal authority - of the special character and features of the computer network within which Cyberpayment systems operate. In particular the CNTO seeks to selectively intercept certain communications and value transfers. Possible situation-specific variations in the design of this kind of investigative instrument are presented in the exercise scenario to illuminate the overall potential of CNTOs - and the associated policy and law enforcement issues.

The concept of a CNTO is described in more detail below. Comparable (and not so comparable) characteristics of CNTOs and GTOs are summarized in Table 4-2.

Table 4.2.

A Comparison of Cyberpayment Network Targeting Orders (CNTOs) and Geographic Targeting Orders (GTOs)

FEATURES	**CNTOs (conceptual)**	**GTOs (as presently configured)**
1. Legal Authority	Bank Secrecy Act	Bank Secrecy Act
2. Zone of Application*	Cyberpayment Instrument, or Issuer-based	Geographical, but may be limited in any capacity
3. Personnel	Few necessary, the capability is built into deployed Cyberpayment systems	Many (Law enforcement personnel must review the captured data).
4. Degree of Automation	High technological intensity	Low-Medium (Artificial Intelligence could be applied to a GTO database)
5. Independent Implementation**	Yes	No

* The *Zone of Application* of CNTOs and GTOs differs fundamentally. GTOs require the physical deployment of personnel and resources for information acquisition. CNTOs would acquire information via Cyberpayment instrument use in: (1) interactions with the issuer and (2) value-transfers that transit known encrypted pathways. Network-based information retrieval tools, such as intelligent software agents, would also allow for the potential pre-positioning of investigative tools within Cyberpayment systems.

** *Independent Implementation* refers to the degree of collaboration that law enforcement authorities must have from businesses involved in funds transfers in investigations of illicit activity. While GTOs require the involvement of financial institutions to collect information on covered transactions, CNTOs would only require that Cyberpayment system issuers design into their systems the ability to conduct network analysis and data collection on electronic value transfers.

It can be seen in the more detailed description below that the CNTO technique has two major distinguishing conceptual characteristics:

I. It would be hidden from the user of a stored value instrument in any individual transaction (though mandated by the card purchaser) through its integration into the Cyberpayment network operating software; it may, however, require the involvement of the Cyberpayment system operator and

II. CNTO actions could only be implemented subject to the legal and administrative rules contained in the BSA as defined, and within the appropriate Cyberpayment system oversight regime.

The Technical Features of the CNTO Concept

A CNTO uses the features of the Cyberpayment network operating system to gain access to electronically stored transaction records. The CNTO utilizes features of the network infrastructure currently being built by Cyberpayment issuers, and aspects of the stored value payment instrument. Stored value instruments have both hardware and software components. In a stored value-type smart card, for example, the architecture of the card is designed to facilitate interaction with a merchant stored value terminal, or with an issuer's electronic value transfer instrument. A stored value card contains a log listing the recent value transfer activity. These logs may contain information regarding the amount and timing of particular transfers, and of the identity of recipients (or sources) of value uploads to the stored value instrument.

In an Internet-based system the tagging of "electronic coins" by issuers facilitates the creation of auditable transaction records maintained by the Cyberpayment firms themselves. In the case of a hybrid Cyberpayment instrument usable both on the Internet and as a stored value card, it can be anticipated that a "tagging infrastructure", containing information on funds flows, the identity of initiators and recipients of value transfers, and the location of merchant and consumer electronic transactions, will be present. This infrastructure creates the potential for narrowly targeted computer-based investigations of electronic payment instrument transactional activity.

CNTO-Related Cyberpayment System Features

Two emerging features of Cyberpayment systems may make possible the remote interrogation of transaction records. First, the generation of tags during value transfers means that funds moved from one Cyberpayment instrument to another bear unique markers that reveal information regarding transactions. The second feature of Cyberpayment networks rests on their integration with the open network standards featured within the TCP/IP Internet protocol suite. The possible use of IP (Internet Protocol) "tunneling" techniques (see below) to segregate "value-transfers" from other Internet traffic would enable Cyberpayment systems to ensure the integrity of their links with consumers, and would also present government authorities with a much easier task of tracing suspicious flows of funds associated with drug trafficking and money laundering.

The sheer volume of network traffic presents a daunting challenge to authorities wishing to conduct any kind of surveillance of information flows over the Internet. Demands for privacy by user communities involved in e-mail and electronic commerce over the Internet also limit the acceptability of investigations into the contents of network messages. Reconciling the expectation of privacy on the Internet with legitimate law enforcement concerns for authorized access to sensitive records is difficult, but could be made more acceptable to affected user communities if network traffic could be categorized or "differentiated" according to the character of the data being transmitted. This sort of data differentiation itself begs the question of *how* unstructured network data is to be filtered, allowing for the capture of discrete types of data, and for the secure (and unimpeded) transmission of other data.

IP Tunneling provides one potential means for differentiating value-transfers from generalized Internet traffic, and then subjecting this value flow to sophisticated network analysis and data mining techniques. IP Tunneling creates a virtual network link within the Internet packet-switched network. This virtual network has an initiating point and an endpoint. Because these two points are known, established network audit and traffic analysis tools could be used to measure the volume and nature of information flows. The initiation and termination points of these IP Tunnels are themselves IP (Internet Protocol) addresses. (See Figure 4.5.) Because many networks allocate these addresses dynamically (allocating network connections to users from a collection of available IP addresses), a subset of available IP addresses would have to be set aside for value transfers alone.

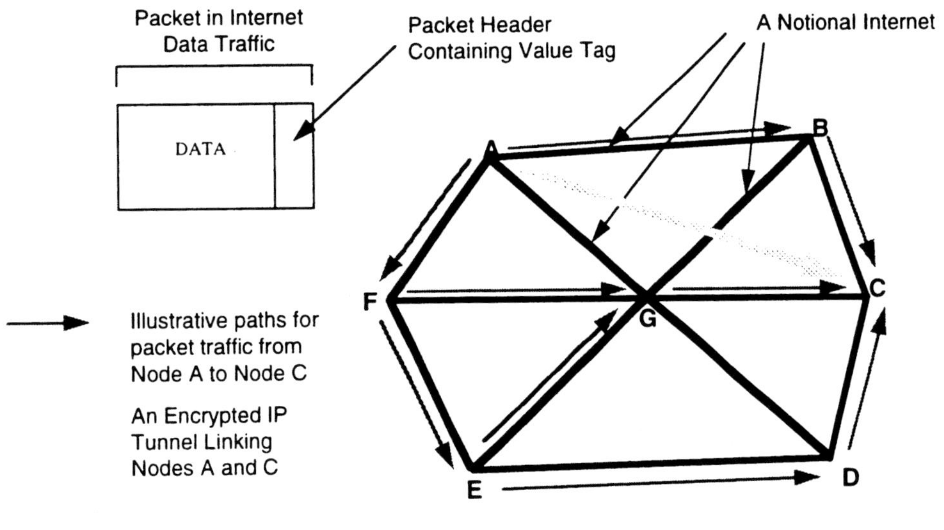

Figure 4.5. The IP Tunneling Concept Applied to Cyberpayment Systems

In the application envisioned for Cyberpayment systems, a tag placed on a value transfer message would invoke a special protocol (termed the Cyberpayment Security Protocol - CSP) within TCP/IP that would itself create a virtual (and encrypted) link between two known IP addresses. The IP Tunnel thus created would be the conduit within which value transfers could be conducted. Servers using TCP/IP with the CSP function built-in would be required to maintain logs of CSP-related network traffic. These records would then be made available to law enforcement and payment system authorities subject to judicial review. One alternative to this requirement would be the generation of "CSP Traffic Reports" by the network operating system itself through an autonomous intelligent agent application. If placed within servers in proximity to CSP-designated IP addresses this application could record value transfers and return the information to secure servers maintained by Cyberpayment oversight authorities.

The CNTO Capability

A CNTO would allow law enforcement authorities to target Cyberpayment instruments suspected of being used by persons for illicit purposes. This illicit use would presumably be embedded within a broader pattern of suspicious activities detected by traditional law enforcement tools and techniques. This fact is critical to an understanding of the CNTO, because it underlines the *complementary* nature of the CNTO contribution to law enforcement investigative capabilities. In this regard, traditional GTOs might be augmented through the use of network information gathering techniques, further facilitating law enforcement information gathering.

A CNTO would not provide "instantaneous" access to transactional data regarding targeted Cyberpayment instruments. Intelligent agent technologies promise a more automated means for gathering information on value transfers. The collection of information from auditable logs, however, would present a challenge in terms of both resources and timeliness. A combination of the two data gathering techniques might produce the best possible information accessibility for oversight authorities.

5. EXERCISE FINDINGS AND ISSUES FOR DECISION MAKING

The exercise participants debated many of the complexities of Cyberpayment system deployment and its impact on government anti-money laundering policies. Discussions were channeled through a preliminary presentation of five issue areas giving an overview of areas and themes impacting Cyberpayment system oversight. In brief, the five areas were: (1) Law Enforcement Issues; (2) Regulatory Issues; (3) International Policy Coordination; (4) Cyberpayment System Architecture and Design Issues; and (5) Definitional Issues.

Participants considered these hypothetical policy issues within a decision-making process linked to the events of the exercise scenario. Their responses were collected by exercise designers and reported to all participants during a discussion session led by the group chairpersons. This information was in turn analyzed by using the participants' annotated briefing books which contained individual responses to the questions presented during the exercises and operational notes taken by conference designers during exercise deliberations.

While no clear consensus on any overall approach to the potential concerns in the Cyberpayment-money laundering nexus was identified during the exercise, an important structuring and focusing of the debate in the five areas did occur. The findings listed below reflect RAND's interpretation of the focused discussion of the participants as well as RAND's independent research.

LAW ENFORCEMENT ISSUES

The discussion of law enforcement issues focused predominantly on the perceived potential value of Cyberpayment instruments to money launderers and others attempting to conceal financial activities from government oversight. The second focus of deliberations was the potential regulatory and law enforcement responses to perceived Cyberpayments abuse, and the place of computer-based investigative techniques alongside more traditional investigative techniques, in countering patterns of abuse.

Issues of jurisdiction, permissible intrusions into individual privacy, and appropriate patterns of international collaboration all impinge upon actions in this area.

As will be clear from the account of deliberations on other topics, government access to Cyberpayment transaction information was a key preoccupation of exercise participants. Established rules governing wiretaps and demands for financial information from regulated financial institutions represented the point of departure for discussions of Cyberpayment-specific issues. One perspective offered within the exercise held that the payment system, and Cyberpayment systems, represented so central an infrastructure to modern society that a special degree of intrusiveness and transparency (from the perspective of oversight authorities and law enforcement) was necessary. In this discussion those who tended to view Cyberpayment value as analogous to currency argued that the government had a unique role in seeing to it that Cyberpayment issuers were subject to the highest levels of government supervision.

From a law enforcement perspective, established patterns of *collaboration* with financial institutions might be reinforced through a routine rewrite of regulations to include the new system characteristics of Cyberpayment networks. A closely guarded interpretation of currently defined legal and regulatory precedent regarding government access to financial records would be used to expand incrementally the purview of law enforcement to cover these new financial products and comparable Information Revolution-based commercial entities. This process and approach, a careful and slow reinterpretation of current anti-money laundering rules and law enforcement investigative procedures, was the one favored by many exercise participants. There was a generalized concern, however, that existing legal and regulatory frameworks could be bypassed by the rapidly evolving nature of Cyberpayment technologies, making piece-meal adaptations to Cyberpayment system realities a potentially dangerous enterprise.

In opposition to a *reactive* law enforcement approach, others argued for close public-private dialogue on the features and characteristics of Cyberpayment instruments and systems. This dialogue, they argued, should include an exchange of views on key issues such as the following:

- Information Accessibility
- Fraud Detection and Surveillance
- International Funds Transfers
- Cyberpayment Instrument Feature Sets

In each of these areas, law enforcement interests in tracking potentially suspicious activities appear to coincide with commercial liability concerns -- offering considerable potential for a collaborative approach to law enforcement within the Cyberpayment area. It is at least possible that this commonality of interest will minimize the necessity for intrusive regulation of the Cyberpayment industry. From this perspective, law enforcement concerns raised outside of a close dialogue with the Cyberpayments industry would remain vulnerable to a critical loss of relevance as they fail to adapt to significant changes in the technical state of the art.

Concerns with individual privacy in Cyberpayment transaction records and the propriety of an expansion in law enforcement surveillance powers to include computer networks also marked the deliberations. Legal conditions governing information access and defining the difference between *classes* of information of relevance to criminal investigations are the critical variables. Divergent perspectives on the permissible role of government in American society dominated this debate.

Those favoring a more limited governmental role in the market place argued for maximal constraints on the government's access to Cyberpayment records. For these participants concerns with consumer privacy and the potential misuse of Cyberpayment information overrode the dangers of potential criminal abuse within Cyberpayment systems.

The contrary perspective saw the potential misuse of Cyberpayment systems by money launderers and others as the principal danger and argued for no unique rules for the protection of Cyberpayment records. Rather, they favored special regulatory treatment for Cyberpayments system records, derivative of the special features of Cyberpayment systems and perceived avenues of misuse that might be exploited by criminals. In such a context, an immediate issue is the relationship of wide-area data capture exercises to more narrow investigations of particular instances of Cyberpayment system abuse.

How are concerns with individual privacy to be reconciled with the potential abuse of relative transaction anonymity by money launderers? As outlined earlier, characterizing patterns of abuse *within* Cyberpayment networks may require the ability to characterize *normal* Cyberpayment system activity in order to establish a baseline for comparison. In this sense, law enforcement activities within the Cyberpayments domain may exceed in scope more traditional investigations of suspected criminal activity within the payment system. This assumes the technical feasibility of computerized intercepts of Cyberpayment value as it transited Cyberpayment networks -- which some participants questioned.

From this perspective, it can be seen that Cyberpayment systems constitute more than challenges to traditional law enforcement methods, they are also a new *technical means* for law enforcement to accomplish entirely traditional investigative activities.

Computer network-based investigative techniques (akin to the hypothetical CNTO construct of the exercise) were seen as having serious potential implications for consumer privacy and established patterns of acceptable law enforcement investigative practice. The issue was whether the disposition of information obtained during such an investigation would pass constitutional examination. It was recognized that the government's use of highly intrusive data-gathering techniques would itself raise profound issues of individual privacy and legitimate law enforcement uses of electronic surveillance.

A particularly provocative issue was the degree to which generalized or "blanket" captures of Cyberpayment transaction data could be used to characterize potentially illegal activity within the payment system. Debate was vigorous between those who argued that targeted examinations of individual records -- with "probable cause" -- should be the basis of Cyberpayment investigations, and others who felt that such data would only be of use if a more general *baseline* of "normal" Cyberpayment System activity had been established through ancillary investigative activities.

REGULATORY ISSUES

During the exercise, regulatory questions were among the most vigorously discussed of the defining concerns involved with Cyberpayment systems. As an overlapping area of interest, regulatory concerns are themselves dependent on more general decisions on both the importance of international policy coordination on the oversight of Cyberpayment systems and the legal character of Cyberpayment value as an economic instrument.

Beginning with an apparently mundane issue -- namely which institutions or entities would have the legal authority to issue Cyberpayment value -- participants voiced a number of differing perspectives on the regulatory issue topic. A majority of participants argued that whichever the regulatory approach was adopted should rest on a collaborative public-private partnership. Under this rubric, however, differences of opinion were voiced on the character and intrusiveness of governmental *mandates* with respect to both Cyberpayment system operators and the electronic payment instruments themselves.

Deliberation focused on two alternative regulatory approaches: one based on issuing entities, the other concentrating on Cyberpayment instrument functionality. In terms of which entities should be able to issue Cyberpayment value, participants split more or less evenly between those arguing that only banks should be allowed to issue value, and those who argued that Money Services Businesses (MSBs) should also be able to participate. The former argued that established financial institutions are already closely regulated with respect to safety and soundness, and that established patterns of cooperation with law enforcement would help to deter and detect occurrences of fraud and abuse within Cyberpayment systems. Other participants extended this argument and maintained that MSBs were also well established within the existing anti-money laundering regime governing financial industry oversight, and asserted that preserving competition required that all issuing institutions be subject to the same rules.

An intermediate position that appeared during deliberations was that any entity willing to operate under the Bank Secrecy Act and/or other applicable regulations should be allowed to issue Cyberpayment value. Such an approach might allow non-traditional financial industry participants to gain a foothold in the Cyberpayments area (e.g., software and telecommunications companies), and increase levels of competition. This position, it was argued, would allow existing regulations governing the payment system to maintain their integrity while decisions were under consideration regarding the ultimate regulatory treatment of the Cyberpayment industry.

In terms of Cyberpayment instrument functionality as appropriate for Cyberpayment system oversight, the following aspects of Cyberpayment instruments were seen as potentially appropriate for governmental regulations:

- Size and Frequency of Peer-to-Peer Value Transfers
- Application Longevity
- Transaction Records
- Stored Value- Smart Card Denomination Limits
- Frequency of Permissible Transactions

In addition, other criteria suggested as potential targets for government regulatory actions were:

- Consumer Privacy and Confidentiality
- Limits on Law Enforcement Access to Information
- Overall Cyberpayment System Stability and Liquidity
- Consumer Protection.

The first five areas cited above all address technical characteristics of network-based and smart-card-type Cyberpayment instruments. These characteristics will likely be set at particular levels by issuers according to traditional standards. The second set of concerns cited, however, involve societal decisions regarding appropriate levels of consumer privacy, permissible law enforcement access to private records, and overall payment system management and predictability. These issues were the subjects of lively debate among exercise participants with a wide range of opinions being expressed.

Some participants expressed the view that Cyberpayment systems, and the records that they necessarily generated, should be subject to the same rules and regulations as more traditional bank records and communications using electronic systems. As observed in this chapter, the law enforcement and government oversight implications of design choices within Cyberpayment systems are critical to future regulatory possibilities. In this sense, design and standards setting in this area appears to warrant significant government attention, if only to assure that the features of deployed Cyberpayment systems do not foreclose information access possibilities.

INTERNATIONAL POLICY COORDINATION

The discussion on international policy issues raised by the Cyberpayment systems focused on the degree to which national rules and regulations on system characteristics could be overturned by international variation in oversight regulation pertaining to anti-money controls.

Participants agreed that Cyberpayment products were inherently international in nature, and that any longer-term regulatory responses would of necessity be international in scope. Differences were expressed, however, regarding the centrality of government-to-government discussions (or even negotiations) regarding common approaches to Cyberpayment system oversight. Some participants argued that the international joint ventures underlying Cyberpayments systems would naturally lead to convergent technical and operational standards. It was further argued that these standards would produce -- or be consistent with -- common approaches to fraud detection and anti-abuse procedures. From this perspective the global nature of Cyberpayment systems will produce market-based anti-fraud and anti-abuse regulatory frameworks requiring relatively little overt governmental participation.

Others maintained that the closeness of Cyberpayment value to currency argued for a more thoroughgoing governmental role in system oversight. With the premise that government may speak on behalf of a *societal interest* in Cyberpayment system safety and soundness, some argued that government must impose some standards -- at least on issuing institutions.

Also from this perspective, the increasingly globalized economic environment raises the issue of harmonization of trade rules (for goods and services) as a means of fostering greater economic growth and efficiency. The potentially positive contribution of Cyberpayment systems to such objectives was also raised as a rationale for a more pro-active governmental role in constructing an international Cyberpayment oversight regime.

However, governmental intervention (through negotiated or discussion-driven international fora) represents a *defensive* response to counter any anti-openness policies, which could damage the competitiveness of U.S.-based Cyberpayment issuers. Participants arguing from this perspective maintained that any government-to-government discussions on Cyberpayment systems should seek to harmonize *downward* (in terms of restrictiveness) any regulations regarding system operations -- with the important exception that safety and soundness concerns should be maintained at a robust level in all issuing countries.

U.S. leadership within international agencies was seen as important to the accomplishment of either overt or more advisory oversight regime initiatives. Again, exercise participants described such initiatives in terms both defensive and more intrusive approaches. It was mentioned frequently that any potential U.S. international action in this area should also cope with problems like securities fraud and the broader safety and soundness of the international infrastructure.

CYBERPAYMENT SYSTEM ARCHITECTURE AND DESIGN ISSUES

The discussion of Cyberpayment systems examined the question of whether this type of payment instrument was a generalized problem for law enforcement and payment system regulators, or whether particular types of Cyberpayment products constituted unique risks of abuse and misuse. Participants did not articulate a consensus on this subject, other than a general observation that *for their own reasons Cyberpayment system operators would tend to invest heavily in designing systems that minimized their degree of exposure to fraudulent use*. This position was extended to argue for a collaborative standards-based approach to regulatory action in the area of system soundness and safety.

Many participants argued strongly that Cyberpayment system operators should be free to select any system architecture (network-based or stored value-card in character, or some fusion of the two types) and payment instrument feature set (i.e., Peer-to-Peer functionality and high denomination limits), so long as they were able to meet governmental standards of regulator and law enforcement transparency and issuer safety and soundness. From this perspective, the determination of product type is best set by the free market, with overall Cyberpayment oversight issues addressed in a fashion which reflects societal concerns with safety and security.

This approach was questioned by some participants who asserted that in seeking to pursue a "hands off" policy on product type, the government would "back into" intrusive oversight because of concerns with potential abuse deriving from particular Cyberpayment instrument characteristics (i.e., the relative anonymity of Cyberpayment value transfers conducted on a Peer-to-Peer basis). From this perspective the government's hands-off posture would need to be changed to develop measures of effectiveness for both traditional and computer-based payment system investigative techniques.

Some participants observed that computer-based techniques would hold a potentially important advantage in investigations due to the quantifiable and reproducible nature of much of the data. Others argued, however, that such information would only be useful if used in a complementary fashion with traditional investigative techniques. This issue arose in the exercise scenario when a decision on whether to use purely computer-based techniques or such investigative tools alongside traditional means arose. Most participants favored the use of both sets of investigative tools with considerable skepticism expressed regarding sustaining the value of traditional law enforcement anti-money laundering techniques. Another argument consistent with this position was that the government would need to articulate *in the near term* a policy on the encryption schemes acceptable for deployment within the Cyberpayment industry.

Participants expressed strong differences on the issue of whether government legal requirements on encryption had any place within the Cyberpayments domain. One perspective argued for governmental encouragement of the highest possible encryption protection for the Cyberpayments industry. Preserving the safety and soundness of Cyberpayment value issuers was the principal rationale for supporters of this position. It was also argued that as long as the government enjoyed assured access to Cyberpayment records *under established legal procedures* the deployment of strong encryption products within Cyberpayment applications could be positively encouraged. Those favoring this position differed on the extent to which government legal requirements would be useful in achieving the undoubtedly positive end of high levels of security in Cyberpayment networks.

The alternate view was that a governmental position on encryption standards for Cyberpayment products was premature, and that in any case the overall societal debate on such issues was nowhere near closure. Adopting an overt position in the short-run would unduly influence the market-driven selection of encryption and other technical features of Cyberpayment products. It was argued that the market should decide these issues in the short-term and that only following a potentially lengthy "shake-out" process would such decisions be appropriate for public sector authorities. The international elements of this issue were also the subject of considerable debate, with a general consensus emerging that any standards reached within the United States should be mirrored in the international community for them to have any enduring validity or relevance.

DEFINITIONAL ISSUES

The issue of how Cyberpayment value is to be defined was vigorously discussed. The debate was framed by the concern with establishing an appropriate regulatory oversight regime for Cyberpayment systems, while at the same time not imposing onerous (and costly) requirements on a maturing industry.

Within the context of anti-money laundering policy, some participants favored the inclusion of emergent Cyberpayment systems under the current Bank Secrecy Act with Cyberpayment value to be defined as equivalent to traditional circulating paper currency (i.e., cash). It was observed that the existing regulatory environment was already establishing customary rules -- on an incremental basis -- that would establish the setting for different Cyberpayment system models. In this area, draft regulations promulgated under the Bank Secrecy Act already affect entities involved in Cyberpayment product tests, as well as those likely to consider the deployment of such products in the future. It was generally felt that related regulatory decisions should be made with an eye to not disadvantaging (or advantaging) any particular Cyberpayment system type, but rather that the marketplace should be allowed to make the determination.

In terms of short and long run decision-making necessities on this subject, differences emerged as to the degree to which current decisions could be isolated from a longer-term determination of regulatory style in the Cyberpayment domain. Some argued that as an entirely new form of value transfer vehicle, Cyberpayment value necessitated an entirely new treatment from the regulatory and law enforcement standpoints. Others argued that even if this were true, short-run decisions would be made in the context of existing laws and perceived problems. These participants sought to reframe the debate in the following terms: What is the appropriate oversight model for Cyberpayment value viewed as an analog to cash? This was contrasted to the question of what the correct model might be if Cyberpayment value were viewed as some other type of consumer-level electronic payment products or services. Finally, some participants argued that decisions made prematurely in the short-run could actually impede longer-term policymaking on the unique characteristics of Cyberpayment systems and counseled caution in the design of "interim" solutions to difficult law enforcement or regulatory questions.

Discussions also extended to those features of Cyberpayment products, (i.e., the high theoretical velocity of electronic value circulation, the relative anonymity of transactions, low or zero levels of transactions costs, and unprecedented transaction volume) of potential utility for money launderers and others seeking to conceal financial activities from governmental authorities. In this contract, consistent with the concern with not imposing additional costs on industry, or disadvantaging any particular Cyberpayment models, some argued that *product types* should be the basic unit of concern (i.e., products offering peer-to-peer functionality, or those offering a relatively high degree of payer anonymity), with only a small number of general regulations applying to all Cyberpayment instruments. If the features of the Cyberpayment instrument were the most important new facts, it was argued, these features should be targeted as narrowly as possible in order to mitigate any potential fraud or abuse. Alternately, others held that the novel features of Cyberpayment instruments posed highly unique regulatory and law enforcement challenges. In this sense, traditional regulatory and law enforcement methods were found particularly wanting. Disagreements were present on estimates of the rapidity with which these challenges would become real, but few doubted that a potentially very important change in the consumer-level payments system could be about to occur.

Differences in perspective on the precise definition of what constitutes Cyberpayment value were thus correlated with different estimates as to the timing of the Cyberpayment challenge to existing regulatory and law enforcement frameworks and according to the extent of anticipated uniformity of different Cyberpayment products. It was argued by some that a fuller appreciation of the electronic nature of the new payment products would allow for much more objective and technically advanced system oversight procedures. An analogy was made with the New York Stock Exchange and NASDAQ with respect to the potentially large contribution that computer-based investigative techniques might make to Cyberpayment system oversight. Defined as a cash equivalent, Cyberpayment systems hold considerable uncertainty with respect to both regulatory and law enforcement impact. At the same time the definition -- or legal and regulatory status -- of Cyberpayment value relative to other electronic and traditional payment products, remains a critical issue for the ultimate determination of the appropriate Cyberpayment oversight regime.

CONVERGENT PERSPECTIVES ON CYBERPAYMENT SYSTEM OVERSIGHT

Discussions during the exercise yielded a wide-ranging set of perspectives on the scale and significance of the Cyberpayment challenge to law enforcement anti-money laundering policies. These perspectives almost of necessity also articulated positions on the appropriate governmental regime for conducting oversight of the emerging Cyberpayment industry. Discussions of appropriate public and private sector roles both converged and diverged on the issue of whether Cyberpayment value was to be treated as an equivalent to traditional currency (i.e. Cash). Positions on this issue were an excellent predictor of subsequent positions on governmental roles in standards setting, international coordination of legal rules, and provisions governing law enforcement's access to transactional information. While a wide-range of debate occurred, three discernible schools -- or approaches -- to Cyberpayment systems were evident.

Schools of Thought in Cyberpayment System Oversight

RAND's analysis of exercise deliberations identified three schools of thought with respect to Cyberpayment system oversight. The following labels refer to these schools below:

Model 1: "Government Lead"
Model 2: "Collaborative"
Model 3: "Self-Regulatory"

The three approaches to Cyberpayment system anti-money laundering oversight differ in many ways, but the central differences stem from the perceived appropriateness of independent governmental action in setting mandates for Cyberpayment systems. Indeed, the overwhelming consensus among exercise participants was in favor of collaborative regulation of Cyberpayment systems — with industry and government sharing the central roles of defining standards and policing fraud and abuse. One interesting omission in most of the discussions was the absence of a significant perceived role for public interest advocates in the construction of the oversight regime. The highly negative perspective on government mandates broke down somewhat when the question of whether a necessary identity of interests could be assumed between business and government. In this area many argued that an irreducible minimum *societal interest* existed that may conflict with the commercial preferences of Cyberpayment issuers.

From this position grew a further debate on the appropriate *timing* of government action. Because the Cyberpayment industry was seen to be maturing, there was a general consensus that whatever regulations that were drafted should not be put in place until the market had more fully developed. More directly, the process through which regulations were designed and made subject to public comment and criticism was identified as a critical issue. The central point of debate seemed to be on the degree of collaboration between business and government in the drafting of regulations governing the Cyberpayment industry. Those arguing for Model 1 viewed it as important that government maintain an entirely "arms length" relationship with the industry. Central features of the Model 1 control perspective are:

- Highly structured and rule-governed contacts between industry and government;
- Direct government-to-government negotiation of harmonized rules for international Cyberpayment anti-money laundering oversight, which would then be drafted into regulations governing national firms;
- Government mandates for procedural and technical standards to be used within Cyberpayment systems, with law enforcement and payment system regulatory requirements for information and transparency the principal drivers of regulatory design;
- Mandates governing the features of particular Cyberpayment products would be imposed reflecting the concerns of law enforcement regarding potential misuse of Cyberpayment systems for criminal purposes;
- All Cyberpayment systems would operate under close government supervision because they are perceived to be issuing Cyberpayment value — which some hold is fully analogous to traditional currency;

Those arguing this perspective are decidedly unconvinced by calls for increased deregulation of the financial industry, and instead perceive a need to prevent a potentially catastrophic degradation in the utility of traditional regulatory and law enforcement tools for fighting payment system abuse.

Model 2 offers a similar but slightly different approach to Cyberpayment system oversight. The central difference between this approach and the one outlined above is that most of the government mandates would derive from a structured process of public consultation where Cyberpayment industry representatives and the broader public would have the right to argue their positions before an administrative board or committee. To summarize this approach:

- A moderately loose process for consultations between industry and government on prospective regulatory action affecting Cyberpayment systems;
- Direct government-to-government negotiation of harmonized rules for international Cyberpayment oversight would be paralleled by a process of industry consultations on prospective rule changes;
- Government mandates for procedural and technical standards to be used within Cyberpayment systems would be weak, perhaps only involving those systems used by government agencies for payments. Law enforcement and payment system regulators would remain the most significant articulators of the governments concerns with Cyberpayment system oversight;
- Cyberpayment systems would operate under a fixed set of rules administered by an independent oversight agency;

Model 3 represents something of a middle ground between the weak and strong variants of traditional governmental oversight. Rather than seeking to impose regulations (deriving from either domestic rule making or international negotiation) on the Cyberpayment industry, this model is based on close collaboration with the private sector on both technical standards and rule making.

The principal features of this approach are:

- Close government-industry collaboration on setting rules governing entities permitted to operate as issuers of Cyberpayment value. An industry-level body might well become the principal partner of government in constructing a flexible and coherent regulatory framework for Cyberpayment systems;
- Oversight is inherently international in scope. This would mean that industry would be represented within governmental fora where international negotiating positions on Cyberpayment standards and oversight were crafted. The government might also elect to allow industry to set its own standards within internationally constituted standards organizations. In this case only broad governmental requirements for safety and soundness concerns would need to be mandated.
- Emphasis is placed on appropriate procedural and technical standards in the underlying infrastructure of Cyberpayment systems. Because these are determined principally by economic and technological factors, government would refrain from setting explicit technical or procedural requirements, instead focusing on overall information access mandates and broad operating standards;

- Qualitative differentiation of applications within the Cyberpayment environment is critical, with different regulatory treatment appropriate for each. This approach argues that a single regulatory regime for all Cyberpayment products is not advisable, and that more qualitatively sensitive decisions must be made regarding the perceived vulnerabilities of particular products to fraud and abuse;
- Government mandates are the last resort for regulation of Cyberpayment products.

Table 5.1.

Findings versus Oversight Principles in Cyberpayment Systems

Oversight Principle	Model One	Model Two	Model Three
Self-Regulatory			X
Collaborative		X	
Government Lead	X		

Table 5.1 captures the essential differences in perspective of the various schools. Model One is the perspective most "friendly" to an expanded regulatory role for government in supervising Cyberpayment systems, with Models 2 and 3 representing the most deregulated forms of Cyberpayment system oversight. Without prejudice to the issue of which model is the most suitable to emerging Cyberpayment systems, it appears clear that Model 1 conflicts the most with contemporary trends favoring the deregulation of the financial services industry. Model 2 could be interpreted as a transitional stage, where models of industry-government collaboration could provide a "proof of principle" for concepts of industry self-regulation and governmental "arms length" supervision. This interpretation would leave Model 3 as an oversight framework perhaps best suited for a mature and well-understood Cyberpayments industry. With established frameworks of industry-government and inter-governmental information and knowledge sharing, it is possible that this sort of oversight model could allow for the reconciliation of market efficiency and competitiveness concerns with public issues regarding the safety and soundness of an emerging payments industry.

6. CONCLUSIONS

CONTRASTING ACTION PLANS FOR CYBERPAYMENT SYSTEM OVERSIGHT

As described in the previous chapter, the RAND exercise helped identify three exemplary action plan architectures consistent with each of the three models of Cyberpayment system oversight.

These exemplary action plans and models reflect differing participant perspectives on the role of government in Cyberpayment system oversight, the potential for industry self-regulation, and the difficulties of designing regulatory guidelines for a brand new industry.

RAND's analysis of participant deliberations have been categorized into three broad schools, or models, of potential Cyberpayment System Oversight. While a consensus on any one of the approaches was lacking, debate returned again and again to the general themes reflected in the models.

In providing examples of policies that such alternative approaches might foster, it is important to emphasize that these models are not mutually exclusive, but rather related to one another through key assumptions as to the pace and character with which the Cyberpayment challenge will emerge. Combinations of these approaches will most likely be visible in actual decision making on the appropriate oversight regime for Cyberpayment systems. It is important to point out, however, that controversies over whether government or industry are best suited to regulate this maturing industry are not ended by the adoption of any particular perspective on Cyberpayment system regulation. The *process* through which these controversies are to be resolved may in fact be of greater importance than the particular end-point argued by proponents of any of the models in question.

The divergent schools of Cyberpayment system oversight do share some common features. First, each of them seeks to assess the applicability of current anti-money laundering rules and regulations to the new payment environment. Definitions of cash or cash equivalence carried to the Cyberpayment domain may guide some to consider only minor modifications to current legislative and regulatory models for Cyberpayment system oversight. A second feature of the debate on appropriate Cyberpayment oversight frameworks is broad agreement on the effectiveness of deregulation in increasing competition and generating innovation in the banking and financial services industries. This fact shifts the balance in the broader debate toward Models 2 and 3 as potential alternative frameworks for government action in the Cyberpayments area. A comparison of these two models reveals that their principal difference is in the number and quality of formal mandates in regulation of Cyberpayment systems.

In Model 3, mandates are a last resort if industry-led standards and procedural rule setting is perceived to have failed. In one sense, this model assumes that — until demonstrated otherwise — industry is best suited to organizing and structuring the development of sound and safe business practices. Government action would only proceed following the *failure* of industry measures to prevent significant abuse. Another difference as compared to the other two models is in the process through which international collaboration on standards setting and oversight coordination would take place. Model 3 argues for the standards setting collaboration by industry-centered standards bodies. Government would craft broad policy guidance, but even this process would be a bilateral dialogue where Cyberpayment issuers (U.S. — based) would negotiate a regulatory environment with regulatory agencies. This regime would then provide the principal negotiating guidance for private-sector dominated discussions within standards bodies.

Model 2 follows a more traditional government-centered regulatory approach, with wide opportunities for public comment on prospective regulations and government to government negotiation of international standards. This approach would also provide a relatively familiar framework for law enforcement to gain access to Cyberpayment system records. This framework would resemble current proposals for a modified Encryption Key Escrow — or Encryption Key Recovery -- model, and would designate a (regulated) third party who would hold keys or coordinate a process of key recovery, for private keys giving access to encrypted Cyberpayment data.

Both of these approaches embrace an interim definition of Cyberpayment value as equivalent to cash. Over the long term, however, these models diverge on the issue of whether governments or the private sector is best suited to overseeing a global Cyberpayment system.

CANDIDATE ACTION PLANS

Listed below are candidate plans that could be considered for each in an attempt to shape constructively the emerging Cyberpayment system environment. Consistent with the debate among exercise participants, the plans and the models do not represent mutually exclusive approaches. The different perspectives are linked by critical assumptions such as the timing of Cyberpayment system deployments by private industry, and on the pace and character of consumer acceptance of the new payment instruments.

Model 1: Government Lead. Cyberpayment oversight could include a strong role for government in directing industry responses to potential Cyberpayment system vulnerabilities. This approach to oversight would anticipate only a few highly structured occasions where industry would be allowed to react to prospective rules.

Model 1 Candidate Plan

I. Issue an administrative finding that Cyberpayment value is to be treated as a cash equivalent for the purposes of payment system oversight.

II. Identify key Cyberpayment system features and begin a regulation writing process designed to bring these payment instruments into close scrutiny. Regulations drafted during this process would include:

- A definition of Cyberpayment instrument functionality including: denomination limits, peer-to-peer value transfer capabilities, system interoperability, and transaction frequency;

- Rules on the permissible issuers of Cyberpayment value;

- Mandates on the technologies contained in Cyberpayment instruments; and
- Mandates on system-audit and remote system management (under legal supervision) capabilities.

III. Initiate preparation of an international meeting involving senior finance ministry officials with a view to creating an international convention on the operation of Cyberpayment systems. Preparatory work would seek to establish common regulatory treatment of Cyberpayment issuers in all participating countries; to work out procedures to ensure the ability of states to enforce legal orders against Cyberpayment issuers or instrument holders whatever their country of residence; and to coordinate law enforcement action against international crime groups;

IV. The Administration would propose legislation, when necessary, establishing federal primacy in the oversight of Cyberpayment systems, and establishing tampering with Cyberpayment instruments (network or card-based) as a federal crime analogous to counterfeiting.

Model 2: Collaborative. This model emphasizes a more collaborative public-private sector partnership in Cyberpayment system oversight. The model envisions expanded governmental consultations with Cyberpayment system operators as the basis for regulatory action. Technical standards within Cyberpayment products would be decided by industry with government mandates only existing for systems used by government agencies to deliver services. Under this model, an independent government agency would administer a fixed set of rules governing the industry.

Model 2 Candidate Plan

I. Continue incremental regulatory action on Cyberpayment systems consistent with the pace of their introduction;

II. Begin a structured six-month set of consultations with industry designed to elicit input for a draft policy paper on Cyberpayment system oversight. The paper would address technology, regulatory, and law enforcement issues in both domestic and international dimensions. This paper would also support the U.S. negotiating position at the proposed meeting to establish an international convention on Cyberpayments system oversight. Industry and government officials would be equally represented in a steering committee through which the policy paper would be drafted.

III. Initiate experts meetings within the G-7 FATF or other international groups to discuss a short-list of the most pressing money laundering concerns of Cyberpayment systems from the point of view of payment system regulators and law enforcement authorities. These meetings would support a major international conference two years hence, at which senior finance ministry officials would be asked to draft a statement on the international oversight of Cyberpayment systems.

IV. Consult Cyberpayment industry representatives on the technical features necessary to establish CNTO-like system interrogation capabilities within planned Cyberpayment networks. Begin a regulation writing process in consultation with privacy advocates to mandate such capabilities for Cyberpayment systems if contacts with industry do not yield desired results.

V. Begin consultations where necessary with the U.S. Congress on the drafting of legal guidelines for law enforcement access to Cyberpayment records. In the interim, establish administrative guidelines for the use of these records by law enforcement authorities in criminal investigations.

Model 3: Self-Regulatory. Industry would be charged with conducting self-regulation under this regime, with government authorized to oversee a new industry self-regulatory organization to ensure effective supervision and enforcement of anti-money laundering controls. International oversight of Cyberpayment systems would take place on a government-to-government basis, but with industry enjoying key representation in governmental bodies charged with drafting positions for international negotiations on Cyberpayment standards and oversight.

Model 3 Candidate Plan

I. Initiate a series of consultations with Cyberpayment industry representatives with a view to encouraging the establishment of an industry-wide association to represent commercial concerns in policymaking.

II. Seek legislation assigning functional responsibility for Cyberpayment systems to an established agency or new administrative body. A board made up equally of industry and government representatives would coordinate regulations in this functional area.

III. The Cyberpayment industry would be asked to provide – on demand – Cyberpayment records for government as needed during criminal investigations. This information access would be governed by administrative guidelines set up by the independent Cyberpayment oversight body, and would not be subject to judicial review.

It appeared that Model 1 conflicted the most with the contemporary trend which favors allowing the market to develop more fully before a regulatory scheme is adopted. Model 2 could be interpreted as a transitional stage, where models of industry-government collaboration could provide a "proof of principle" for concepts of industry self-regulation and governmental "arms length" supervision. This interpretation would leave Model 3 as an oversight framework perhaps best-suited when the market has matured. With established frameworks of industry-government and inter-governmental information and knowledge sharing, it is possible that this sort of oversight model could allow for the reconciliation of market efficiency and competitiveness concerns with public issues regarding financial privacy and the safety and soundness of the Cyberpayment industry.

The material that follows looks first at the common action elements that might be included in a preparatory phase to any government oversight approach.

Common Elements

The introduction of Cyberpayment systems raises potential concerns in five areas: (1) law enforcement issues; (2) regulatory issues; (3) need for international policy coordination; (4) Cyberpayment system architecture and design issues; and (5) traditional definitions of currency. Work in any area would necessitate essential *preparatory activity* for any more overarching regulatory project aimed at influencing Cyberpayment industry trends. A common preparatory phase of government action to guard against illicit uses of these systems could include:

- Conducting a baseline analysis of the technologies being used in proposed Cyberpayment system designs. This analysis would address: (1) the potential vulnerability of proposed technologies to "hacker" attack; (2) the ability of the system to deliver information on Cyberpayment value transfers to auditors; (3) the privacy implications of different Cyberpayment system architectures.

- Asking Banks and Money Service Businesses interested in operating Cyberpayment systems to respond to a list of security and abuse concerns generated by law enforcement and payment system regulators. Required responses would address the critical information access concerns of the government in anticipation of broad deployment of Cyberpayment systems, and to react to scenario-based insights regarding potential patterns of abuse by criminals.

- Collecting and analyzing the results of the Cyberpayment industry submissions prior to the release of a preliminary policy paper by the U.S. Government (agency or agencies to be decided) that would constitute an initial government statement of regulatory preferences on Cyberpayment systems.

- Calling a special meeting of the FATF or some other international group, in order to begin structured experts meetings to discuss the technical standards and law enforcement issues raised by the emergence of Cyberpayment systems. This activity would be designed to coordinate with the U.S.-initiated Cyberpayment issuer requirement listed above.

- Convening a major conference involving senior Cyberpayment industry representatives, senior staff from the law enforcement community and potential payment system regulatory agencies, and international observers from international financial institutions as a final activity prior to the initiation of a formally introduced Cyberpayment oversight policy. The objective of such a conference would be to achieve a degree of consensus on the character of emerging Cyberpayment systems, a consciousness of common regulatory and law enforcement challenges, and – where possible – agreement on the elements of a strategy for conducting international oversight of Cyberpayment systems.

Candidate plans for addressing the potential problems posed by Cyberpayment systems share many common features. The principle differences among them are in the level of government mandates imposed upon Cyberpayment system operators. In turn, the scope of administrative action also varies, with the Models 1 and 2 seeking a binding international convention on Cyberpayment system oversight, and Model 3 initiating an industry-centered approach whose international version would likely include the largest private global financial institutions managing the sector on behalf of governments.

Combinations of these approaches, rather than any one perspective, are the most likely outcomes given the necessity for consensus-based action. Participants within the exercise considered the merits of government and industry-led actions to counter perceived Cyberpayment system vulnerabilities. While no clear consensus emerged, the predominant perspective in the deliberations supported close industry-government collaboration to address potential problems.

PREPARATION FOR ACTION

Participants in the exercise, whatever their particular positions on the action to be taken, did broadly share the idea that government needed to begin thinking of the appropriate regulatory and law enforcement actions necessary to adapt effectively to emerging Cyberpayment systems. Because new technologies are currently under pilot testing, government already confronts the potential need to include Cyberpayment system operators under existing regulations. This inclusion has been achieved through the creative extension of current anti-money laundering requirements of banks and MSBs to those seeking to deploy Cyberpayment products.

Analysis of the technologies and features of the new electronic payment systems is the first step toward understanding their implications for traditional oversight rules. The entities most aware of the fast-changing technical state of the art are -- not surprisingly -- the commercial firms designing Cyberpayment products. Consequently, it is advisable that government expand the dialogue with the private sector on the character of Cyberpayment products, including the security-related technical details intended to protect the safety and soundness of Cyberpayment systems. Information gained during this process could contribute to a thoroughgoing evaluation of the appropriate policy environment for Cyberpayment products.

A BOTTOM LINE

What overall conclusions can be drawn from RAND's analysis of Cyberpayment systems and money laundering? The exercise experience revealed a wide scope of issues facing potential payment system regulators and the law enforcement community.

Prompt collaborative action by industry and government and among governments to prevent the exploitation of Cyberpayment system vulnerabilities is a critical way to respond to this still-nascent threat. Collaboration on standards, regulatory transparency, and vigorous surveillance of possible vulnerability exploitation offers the key to successful protection of Cyberpayment systems from abuse. Furthermore, the scope of the potential money laundering problem is international. Effective law enforcement will require national governments to collaborate in setting the ground rules for Cyberpayment systems' deployment and operation.

The exercise provided a valuable arena in which policy and law enforcement issues raised by Cyberpayment systems could be examined. In the future, an extension of the simulation to include international participants would allow for a deeper understanding of the challenges involved. In turn, the exercise highlighted the importance of a harmonization of approaches to

Cyberpayment system oversight. The danger that criminals will seek to exploit weaknesses in regulations wherever they appear suggests that governments need to coordinate investigative and enforcement activities aimed at minimizing potential abuse.

While it is premature to draft a comprehensive regulatory regime for Cyberpayment products, a structured dialogue involving government, issuing companies, and other stakeholders, will help to shape the direction of any such regime. The authors hope that the insights outlined in this report will assist in the advancement of public debate on Cyberpayment system security and the appropriate role for government in this rapidly growing segment of the Global Information Infrastructure.

APPENDIX A. "THE DAY AFTER..." METHODOLOGY

To carry out this research effort, RAND relied heavily on an exercise-based framing and analysis of Cyberpayment system security issues and participation in the exercise by a diverse set of stakeholders from government and industry. The diversity of stakeholders affected by the emergence of a new type of electronic payment instrument suggests that a wide-range of interests and perspectives will likely exist on the appropriate level and kinds of governmental oversight for such an instrument. The exercise methodology employed is designed to draw out and address issues on such wide-ranging and dynamic strategy and policy landscapes.

RAND employed a previously developed exercise methodology, called "The Day After...," as the vehicle for this framing and analysis of potential Cyberpayment system misuse. This methodology relies on a three-step policy and strategy exploration exercise in which participants are first presented with hypothetical future crises and asked to develop appropriate responses to such crises, and then asked to consider possible near-term action elements in the wake of that experience.

During step one of the exercise ("The Day Of..."), participants are presented with a change or foreshadowed change in the international economic and political environment. Step two concerns "The Day After..." — the aftermath of a major strategic crisis affecting Cyberpayment systems and established patterns of governmental oversight. Step three returns to the "The Day Before..." and considers measures that could mitigate many of the worst potential Cyberpayment system vulnerabilities, and allow for the coordination of national and possibly international law enforcement and payment system action to combat criminal abuse of Cyberpayment systems.

As described in more detail below, the so-called operational phase of the exercise process consisted of two exercises in May and June of 1997 involving roughly 100 government and industry participants. Through the exercise process, these participants assessed possible adverse implications for information technology and applications and addressed unresolved issues associated with the limitations of traditional policy and law enforcement responses to the potential abuse of Cyberpayment systems by international organized crime groups. Participants were put in a position where they could see with greater clarity the challenge of planning appropriate policy and law enforcement responses to Cyberpayment security problems that would not impede industry deployment of new payment system technologies, or unduly diminish the competitiveness of U.S. firms relative to foreign Cyberpayment system operators.

THE EXERCISE

Participants prepared for the exercise with materials read at home and a set of preliminary briefings at the exercise. After the briefings, participants broke into independent groups (in one operational case, five groups and the other six groups) and proceeded through the basic steps in the "The Day After..." methodology. Under the leadership of a chairperson, each of the groups followed the identical three-step exercise, comparing the results of their deliberations in two plenary "reporting" out sessions that occurred after the second step and at the conclusion of the exercise.

Participants were not expected to represent the views of their own or any other agency, office, corporation or organization. Rather, they were asked to assume the role of advisors to senior-level government decision-makers (or a decision-making body) in a group deliberative process in advance of a formal decision-making meeting.

The group tasks were two-fold: (1) to finalize a document (an issues and options paper) for an upcoming government decision-making meeting and (2) to make recommendations on those issues in the document where consensus on a specific option or course of action can be achieved.

The first two steps of the exercise (see Figure 5.1) were set in the year 2004. The third step returned to the present or, more precisely, the very near future. The basic steps in the exercise were:

STEP ONE. First phase of the crisis. Competing Mexican and Colombian drug traffickers increasingly exploit Cyberpayment technologies for money laundering. U.S. decision-makers face a series of difficult tactical and strategic issues in the areas of law enforcement, international financial institution collaboration, and bilateral initiatives to improve U.S.-Mexican Cyberpayment system oversight.

STEP TWO. Second phase of the crisis. Escalation in the "Mexican Drug War" and further exploitation of Cyberpayment systems for money laundering by the drug cartels, in spite of more aggressive law enforcement efforts. Cartel efforts threaten the financial and perhaps political stability of Mexico. U.S. decision-makers face a series of crisis-driven international law enforcement and anti-money laundering Cyberpayment issues.

STEP THREE. Return to the present/near future; lessons learned/ implications stage of the exercise. Participants address the challenge of formulating a strategy and policy "Action Plan" that would make the hypothetical events portrayed in the foregoing scenario impossible, less likely, and/or more manageable. The objective is to develop and recommend a set of candidate actions and ideas for: (1) government-industry cooperation and (2) regulatory, law enforcement, and legislative responses to the potential abuse of Cyberpayment systems for money laundering.

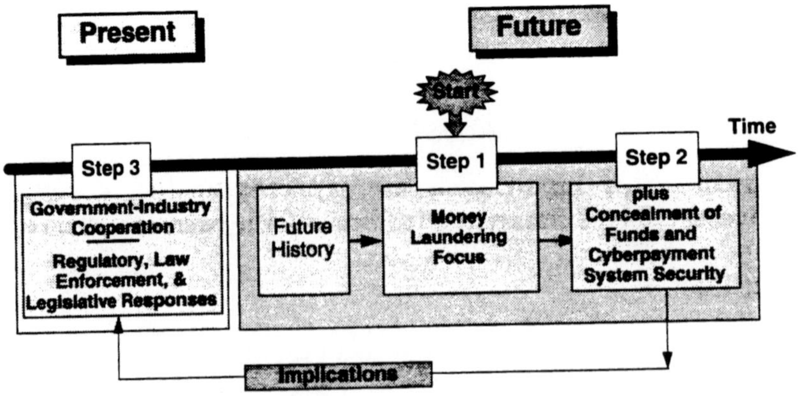

Figure A.1. Exercise Methodology

THE EXERCISE DESIGN PROCESS

RAND recognized at the outset that the exercise faced a particular challenge in the likely need to educate most of the projected exercise participants about both Cyberpayments and money laundering. In light of this, it was decided to build the exercise on a scenario that would have high degree of familiarity to all participants. This led to a scenario based on the prospect that drug cartels could become early adopters of Cyberpayments for money laundering.

The time frame chosen for the scenario was intended to be far enough into the future so that Cyberpayment systems would have progressed substantially, but not so far into the future that the market and technology for such systems were fully mature. The original choice for this date was 2002; the date used in the end was 2004.

In support of this, a "future history" was developed that described:

- Hypothetical developments in Cyberpayment systems; the emergence of criminal exploitation of Cyberpayment systems for money laundering; and international and U.S. responses to this challenge.

- Hypothetical Mexican drug cartel exploitation of Mexican Cyberpayment systems for money laundering in the context of a drug war involving competing Mexican drug cartels both of which seek to suborn the Mexican government's anti-drug and anti-money laundering efforts.

Four tests of the exercise were conducted from January to April 1997 followed by operational exercises in May and June. The testing period provided an opportunity for:

- Exploring time-efficient methods of educating participants about both Cyberpayments and money laundering and their nexus.

- Sharpening the development of Cyberpayment-money laundering issues that might emerge in the context of the chosen Mexican drug cartels scenario.

- Exploring a wide range of ideas on possible U.S. and international responses to the Cyberpayments-money laundering problems in the years between now and 2004.

- Similarly exploring a wide range of ideas on possible U.S. and international responses to Cyberpayments-money laundering problems in crisis.

- Developing ideas on possible strategies and near-term initiatives that might mitigate or even eliminate the kinds of problems portrayed in the scenario.

The final two operational exercises in May and June involved over 100 senior participants from industry, government, and academia. Both the preceding design and testing process and the results from those two exercises constitute the principal basis for this report.

EXERCISE HISTORY

The exercise was developed and employed over a six to seven month period (See Table 5.1). After an initial research and design period, the project employed a series of four structured tests of the exercise and scenario materials. The first test involved RAND and FinCEN personnel from the Washington DC area. The second through fourth tests involved RAND personnel and personnel from FinCEN, other U.S. Department of Treasury personnel, and representatives from the Cyberpayments industry. The scenario examined a drug-cartel generated economic and political crisis in Mexico. The case illuminated potential problems flowing from the possible use of Cyberpayment systems by money launderers working for international narcotics cartels. Participants in the exercise discussed law enforcement and Cyberpayment oversight problems that flowed from the perceived abuse of these systems — and evaluated potential remedial measures for safeguarding Cyberpayment network security.

Exercise materials were refined during the test series, and implemented fully in two operational exercises (See Table A.1) involving senior government personnel representing executive branch agencies involved in Cyberpayment system oversight, and senior corporate officials from the Cyberpayments industry.

Table A.1.

Exercise History

TESTS	PARTICIPANTS
23 January 1997	RAND Washington and FinCEN Staff
20 February 1997	RAND Washington and FinCEN Staff
12 March 1997	U.S. Treasury personnel, academia experts and industry representatives
17 April 1997	Treasury Department and other Executive Branch officials, Congressional Staff
OPERATIONAL	**PARTICIPANTS**
5 May1997	Executive Branch officials, academic experts, senior Cyberpayment Industry officials.
2 June 1997	Executive Branch officials, Congressional staff academic experts, senior Cyberpayment industry officials

The lengthy testing phase allowed for research and design activities to reinforce feedback received from participants in order to improve the quality of the exercise materials. The process also allowed for the assessment and analysis of different perspectives on Cyberpayment problems, and also enabled us to more easily identify emerging schools of thought regarding potential vulnerabilities of Cyberpayment systems, and the appropriate governmental oversight roles for these systems.

APPENDIX B. EXERCISE MATERIALS

FinCEN

Cyberpayment Systems Exercise

Tab G

Exercise Future History (1997-2004)

2 June 1997

RAND

FUTURE HISTORY
Developments in Cyberpayment Systems

In 1999 broadly compatible merchant Smart Card terminals begin to be widely distributed; financial institutions compete in Smart Card functionality	Global economy possibly on brink of major shift to Cyberpayment systems
By 2001 almost all cellphones and personal computers were compatible with Smart Cards	Emerging problem of Cyberpayment system use for money laundering; especially acute re Drug dealers

Developments in Cyberpayment Systems

Many **retailers initially resisted** a **transition to stored value-type Smart Cards** because of **terminal compatibility issues**. However, as a result of "pro-compatibility" efforts by transaction processing system providers, **in 1999 broadly compatible merchant terminals began to be widely distributed. Banks and other financial institutions** quickly began to **compete** in providing various levels of payment-related services and other elements of **functionality in stored value-type Smart Cards and various e-cash systems.**

The expandability of stored value-type Smart Cards fostered rapid innovations in automated payment systems. By 2001 **almost all cell phones** and **personal computers** sold world-wide were **compatible with Smart Cards, effectively merging the Smart Card and e-cash concepts.**

Due to a global transition to chip-based credit cards and accompanying aggressive global marketing efforts by the major credit card conglomerates, an estimated **80 million Smart Cards** were **in use by the end of 2003**. The number of Smart Card users is now expected to double every six months for the next two years.

The rapid adoption of Cyberpayment systems has, however, exposed a number of **critical weaknesses** in **existing legal and regulatory frameworks** and **law enforcement capabilities** for **combating money laundering**. As described below, this problem has become **especially acute in combating money laundering by drug dealers** and others who previously had to launder **large sums of cash** at costs that by 2002 had reached close to thirty percent.

By early 2002, a **series of incidents** had **heightened concern** in the U.S. and the E.U. as to the **extent of the criminal misuse** of Cyberpayment systems - and **the apparent**

increasing potential for currency and national economic destabilization in countries where Cyberpayment systems are not closely regulated. Among the most notable of the incidents that took place are those described below:

> Critical series of Cyberpayment abuse incidents (cont.):
> • (April 2000 in New York) Forest Hills Mercedes dealer indicted for accepting $30 million in drug proceeds in exchange for 200 automobiles; money was loaded in Smart Cards in Panama, taken to Europe, and sent to dealer via wire transfers
> • (September 2000 in Miami) Crack dealer computer contains over $240,000 in stored e-cash; spreadsheet shows history of e-cash transactions with Mexican drug cartel money broker. Drug arrests also yield over 300 large denomination Smart Cards altered to store value above supposed maximums.

• In New York City

In April 2000, the **owner of a Mercedes dealership** in Queens was indicted for allegedly accepting more than **$30 million in Cyberpayment-laundered drug proceeds** in exchange for luxury automobiles. The drug proceeds were initially **pooled as cash in Panama, loaded in increments of $20,000 each into merchant Smart Cards issued by a Panamanian bank,** and **taken by courier to Europe for deposit in a London bank account.** The money came **back to the U.S. through wire transfers** purported to represent business transactions between the Mercedes dealer and a European investment group. The **automobiles** in question were **delivered to a variety of alleged drug cartel principals** in Colombia, Mexico, and Panama.

• In Miami, Florida

In September 2000, agents from the South Florida Organized Crime Drug Enforcement Task Force (OCDETF) serving a **search warrant** on a suspected stash house of a **known crack cocaine dealer** in Coral Gables seized three kilos of powder cocaine, $24,000 in currency, and a computer whose hard drive revealed **electronic purse software containing more than $240,000 in stored e-cash value**. A **spreadsheet** revealed a history of more than $7 million in Internet-based e-cash transactions between the Coral Gables dealer and a **money broker linked to Mexican drug money laundering**.

Two **individuals arrested** at Miami International Airport **in connection with the same operation** were found to be **carrying over 300 large denomination Smart Cards issued by a Mexican bank.** Examination of the cards revealed that almost all of them had been **altered to store more value than their supposed maximum denominations.**

FUTURE HISTORY

Developments in Cyberpayment Systems (cont.)

> Critical series of Cyberpayment abuse incidents (cont.):
> • (October 2000 in Houston) Houston Narcotics Squad officers observe use of Smart Cards and cellphones being used to conduct drug-related transactions; practice quickly becomes widespread
> • (November 2000 in Antigua) Antigua creates "Antiguan Cyberdollars" as new international currency tied to value of the U.S. dollar; unanticipated increase in value of the U.S. dollar plus concerns about Antiguan Cyberdollar integrity leads to a run on Antiguan Cyberdollars and Antiguan insolvency.

• In Houston, Texas

In October 2000, Houston Narcotics Squad officers conducting a **video surveillance of an open air drug market** reported the following incident:

"Customer approaches subject white male on corner of 13th and Richmond Streets. Customer hands subject item which appears to be **small plastic card**. Subject produces **cellular telephone** through which he 'swipes' card. Subject then places **brief telephone call** after which he returns card to customer. Customer crosses street to left front window of residence at 1233 South 13th where he receives small plastic bag containing what appears to be **narcotics**."

Police reports over the next several months contained examples of **similar use of Smart Cards and cell phones** for **drug purchases** in other parts of Texas.

• In Antigua

In November 2000, the Antiguan government began granting **special privileges to foreign corporations** to enter Antigua to **create a new Cyberpayment product - "Antiguan Cyberdollars"** - that would serve as a potentially **new international currency** and make Antigua the leading issuer of regulated Cyberpayment products in the Caribbean. Ignoring U.S. and E.U. cautions, Antigua **exited the Eastern Caribbean monetary system** in favor of the new Cyberpayment instrument and agreed to **guarantee the exchangeability of Antiguan Cyberdollars for a set amount of U.S. currency.**

In March 2001, a **dramatic upward shift in the value of the U.S. dollar** created **serious pressures on the foreign currency reserves of the Antiguan government** as speculators sought to convert their Antiguan electronic currency into U.S. funds. As a result, Antiguan1 foreign exchange reserves were exhausted and Antigua was forced to seek an **emergency loan from the IMF** in order to avoid default on a large segment of its external debt.

Critical series of Cyberpayment abuse incidents (cont.):
- (April 2001 in Phoenix) Grocery store owner admits to accepting Smart Cards from drug transactions which he remits to his bank through his merchant point-of-sale terminal; certified e-cash coins issued back to the grocer are in turn transmitted via the Internet to designated destinations
- (July 2001 in Los Angeles) GTO fails to flush money launderers to bulk export routes. Later report indicates that money launderers moved quickly in marketing Cyberpayment-based money laundering services in the area.

- ***In Phoenix, Arizona***

In April 2001, a **Suspicious Activity Report (SAR) from a bank in Phoenix** reported that a small **grocery store** which had **historically** averaged **$5,000-8,000 per week in Smart Card deposits** had **recently** been processing Smart Card transactions at a rate of **more than $80,000 per week.**

Under questioning by U.S. Customs Service agents, the **grocer** admitted that several times a week an individual would come to his store with a **bag filled with $20-$100 denomination Smart Cards** which had been **accepted for drug purchases by local drug traffickers.** The **grocer** would **download the cards' value to his bank account by** running them through his merchant point-of-sale terminal. The **bank** in turn **issued certified e-cash coins to the grocer.** The **grocer** would then **transmit the e-cash coins** via the Internet based upon **instructions, never forwarding the funds to the same destination twice.** The grocer received a **4% commission** on all transactions.

- ***In Los Angeles***

In July 2001, a **GTO** issued for the LA area imposed **strict new identity validation, record-keeping, and reporting requirements** on money transmitters and other financial service providers **in the region.** In contrast to the 1997 experience with the GTO in New York and the 1998 GTO in Miami, the **"flushing" of would-be money launderers of cash drug proceeds to airports and other bulk export routes** - and resultant apprehension of couriers and seizure of large quantities of cash - **did not take place.**

A later report indicated that **"opportunistic" money launderers** had **moved quickly in marketing Cyberpayment-based money laundering services** in the LA area including both **exchanging Smart Cards for cash** and **transmitting e-coins to foreign accounts.**

FUTURE HISTORY

International and U.S. Responses to the Cyberpayment Challenge

FATF recommends greater regulatory agency coordination: • Sharing of intelligence • Experts forum • Early warning system	U.S. debate on FATF recommendations focuses on nature of Cyberpayments; Proposal to tag all Cyberpayment transactions fails
E.U. summit endorses FATF recommendations; warns of vulnerability of global Cyberpayment system to weak links	

International and U.S. Responses to the Cyberpayment Challenge

In response, in March of 2002, at a meeting in Paris the **Financial Action Task Force (FATF)** recommended an **expansion of regulatory agency coordination** to ensure more effective surveillance and policing of Cyberpayment systems. The countries in attendance agreed to pursue an action agenda to include:

- **Enhanced sharing of intelligence** among Financial Intelligence Units (FIUs);

- Creation of an "**experts forum**" to discuss means by which Cyberpayment systems might be more effectively secured against money laundering;

- Pilot testing of a "**Cyberpayment system abuse early warning system**" that would pool payment system abuse information from all participating countries.

In May 2002, an E.U. summit meeting **unanimously endorsed "rapid implementation" of the FATF recommendations**. A number of E.U. Ministers of Finance cautioned, however, that the **long-term "strengthening" and "harmonizing" of the global Cyberpayment security system** was **vulnerable to other "weak links"** in the emerging system with Russia, Poland, Brazil, Colombia, and Mexico among the countries cited in this regard.

In the **U.S.** there was continued **debate on whether Cyberpayments** should be treated as **akin to traveler's checks or some other monetary instrument** . A proposal to **"tag" all Cyberpayment transactions** to delineate Cyberpayment bit streams from all other "non-currency" bit streams also became **contentious based on privacy issues.** These and other Cyberpayment issues were among the multitude of issues that became **part of the inconclusive 2003 Congressional debate** on revisions to U.S. encryption policy.

FUTURE HISTORY

International and U.S. Responses to the Cyberpayment Challenge (cont.)

<u>Cyberpayment Security Act of 2003</u>

- Authority provided for the use of Cyberpayment NetworK Targeting Orders (CNTOs) under the Bank Secrecy Act
- Any tampering with Smart Card functionality deemed as "cyber-counterfeiting"
- Interagency Financial Crime Coordination Council (FCCC) created

Smart Card "functionality" standards (card longevity, # of transactions recorded, frequency of transactions, maximum amount on a card, etc.) rejected

In the fall of 2003 the U.S. Congress passed a "limited" **<u>Cyberpayment Security Act of 2003</u>**. The legislation's main features:

- Confirming the legitimate use of **Cyberpayment Network Targeting Orders (CNTOs)** under the Bank Secrecy Act.

- Deeming any **tampering with the functionality** of Smart Card systems as **"cyber-counterfeiting" and a Federal offense.**

- Creation of an interagency **Financial Crime Coordination Council (FCCC)** co-chaired by the **Under Secretary of Treasury (Enforcement)** and the **Deputy Attorney General** which included law enforcement elements from Treasury, Justice, and local and regional crime fighting task forces.

Late maneuvering led to deletion of a controversial "Smart Card Functionality" section that would have imposed Smart Card standards on:

- **Card longevity** (i.e., "stale dating" of cards to require reissuance of value)

- **Number of transactions recorded** (i.e., a minimum audit trail)

- **Frequency of transactions** (i.e., limiting certain kinds of repetitious use)

- **Maximum amount on a card** (i.e., limiting the potential for fraud)

FUTURE HISTORY
Cyberpayment Abuse in Mexico

In April 2001 new Tijuana- and Guadalajara- based cartels emerge as dominant in Mexican drug business	"Peace Treaty" between Mexican cartels collapses as Guadalajara Cartel attacks Tijuana Cartel
Tijuana Cartel initiates plan to take over U.S. markets where Guadalajara Cartel had recently gained dominance	U.S. is aided by Tijuana Cartel in widespread drug seizures and exposure of Guadalajara and Cali money laundering operations in U.S.

Cyberpayment Abuse in Mexico

In April 2001, U.S. law enforcement officials monitoring the drug trade in Mexico reported the **emerging dominance of two powerful new Mexican drug Cartels -** a **new Tijuana-based cartel** led by a group of well-educated northern Mexican elites and a **new Cali-backed Guadalajara Cartel -** both capitalizing on the successful 2000 prosecution of the key leaders of the Arellano Felix, Juarez, and Gulf Cartels that had dominated the drug trade in Mexico in the 1990s.

Initially, it **appeared that** the **historical geographic division of the drug market in the U.S. would "keep the peace"** between the two newly dominant cartels - especially in the light of "stabilization campaigns" of unprecedented violence during which both drug cartels had been able to "roll-up" their opponents within Mexico. However, in August of 2001 undercover agents reported that the new **Tijuana cartel** appeared to harbor **new territorial ambitions** that included **U.S. markets where the Guadalajara Cartel had recently gained dominance**. These ambitions were apparently in part rooted in the Tijuana Cartel's establishment of **new sources of supply of cocaine in Peru, Bolivia, and Ecuador.**

In October 2001, the implicit **"peace treaty" between the two new cartels collapsed** with the **assassination of a key leader of the Tijuana Cartel** and the exposure of a **campaign by the Guadalajara Cartel** to enlist corrupt local and Federal Police in northern Mexico in an **effort to strike a "death blow" at the new Tijuana Cartel** before its wide-ranging ambitions could be realized.

In February 2002, **leaks** to U.S. and Mexican drug enforcement authorities **attributed to the Tijuana Cartel** led to **large drug seizures from Florida to Texas**. Arrests made at the time decapitated much of the regional distribution network of the **Guadalajara** cartel in the southern U.S. and **exposed several large Cali and**

Guadalajara money laundering operations involving prestigious banks in Florida, Texas, and Missouri.

In June 2002 anti-establishment reform figure captures Mexican Presidency	Guadalajara Cartel retaliates against Tijuana Cartel; Drug war escalates
Fall 2002: New Mexican gov't - aided by Tijuana Cartel - launches major crack-down on the Guadalajara and Cali Cartels	Mexican Cartel money laundering increasingly focused on Cyberpayments
	DEA operation reveals details of use of e-cash systems for money laundering

In the spring of 2002 a **new and charismatic "anti-establishment" political leader** with a base in central and eastern Mexico **capitalized on domestic outrage at the heavy civilian casualties caused by the then rapidly accelerating Mexican drug war** to mount a challenge against the Presidential candidate of the PRI. In a stunning upset, the anti-establishment candidate **won the Mexican Presidency** in the June 2002 election while his anti-PRI political coalition was able to gain a narrow working majority in the Mexican Congress.

During the fall of 2002, the new **Mexican government** launched a **major crack-down on the Guadalajara Cartel and its Cali allies and supporters** - aided in part by **covert information provided by the Tijuana Cartel.**

In December, the **Guadalajara Cartel** struck back in a **new wave of bombings aimed at the Tijuana Cartel** including the successful bombing of a private airplane which killed the family of the second in command of the Tijuana Cartel.

In January and February of 2003 investigative collaboration between U.S. and Mexican law enforcement authorities revealed that **Mexican drug money laundering operations** - and especially those of the **Tijuana Cartel** - were increasingly **focused on stored value-type Smart Card products and Internet-based payment systems**. A wide spectrum of financial institutions in Mexico, the U.S., the Cayman Islands, Antigua, and Russia were found to be involved in the **receipt and transfer of these funds via cyberspace**.

In one **DEA "storefront" undercover operation,** undercover agents posing as on-line distribution representatives for a major manufacturing company **sold high-value retail goods to Tijuana Cartel associates in exchange for e-cash.** After each transaction the agents were instructed to **transmit the e-coins to an anonymous Internet remailer address**. The experimental use of "value tagging" enabled the agents to trace the flow of funds through various sites back to the cartel agents in Tijuana and Monterey.

FUTURE HISTORY

Cyberpayment Abuse in Mexico (cont.)

In March 2003 at U.S.-Canada-Mexico Summit Mexican President promises bank reform	In December 2003 Mexican law enforcement computer networks found to be compromised by hackers; advanced communications & encryption techniques in use by both cartels
Mexican government reform efforts faltering by summer 2003; severe financial crisis appears imminent	

At a March 2003 summit between the Presidents of Mexico and the United States and the Prime Minister of Canada, the Mexican President promised to pursue a **comprehensive bank reform program** with the intent of "radically reducing the role of the Mexican bank system in North American financial crime."

By mid-summer of 2003, the U.S. had become very alarmed by the continued deterioration of the economic and political situation in Mexico. After an initial "good start," the **Mexican reform program appeared to be faltering** as Cyberpayment abuse in Mexico continued to rise and evidence mounted of an increased lack of public confidence in the government's financial policies.

In early December of 2003 a U.S. anti-money laundering Task Force that was tracking on-line purchases of high-value goods to launder funds discovered that **intelligence being provided to Mexican law enforcement** was being **systematically leaked** to the drug cartels. It was later learned that the **computer networks of Mexican law enforcement agencies** had been **compromised by separate groups of hackers** employed by both the Tijuana and Guadalajara cartels.

FinCEN

Cyberpayment Systems Exercise

Tab H

Exercise STEP ONE

2 June 1997

RAND

Tab H
STEP ONE Situation Report

10-15% discounts to drug customers paying with Smart Cards	Head of Tijuana Cartel nearly assassinated after secret meeting with representatives of the Mexican government
Major offensive in Mexico by well-equipped Mayan insurgents	

Emerging Problems

In San Diego

In early February 2004, undercover narcotics officers reported that drug dealers in the area working for the Tijuana Cartel were beginning to offer **10-15% discounts to customers who paid with Smart Cards.** The rationale given was that the **cost of money laundering for Smart Cards** was **"less than half" that for cash** and **"far less risky."**

In Southern Mexico

In early February of 2004, the **Mayan National Liberation Front** launched a **major offensive in the southern Yucatan** including widespread acts of **sabotage** against government facilities employing **advanced infantry combat equipment** including modern night vision equipment and encrypted satellite phones. Intelligence reaching Washington pointed to the **Guadalajara cartel** as the **principal financial source for the insurgents' growing purchases of modern weaponry.**

In Mexico City

On March 8th, the **head of the Tijuana Cartel** was **nearly killed** in a car bomb explosion **three hours after a supposedly secret meeting with representatives of the Mexican Government.** His presence in the city had previously prompted a wide-spread rumor of a government attempt to reach an "understanding" with the Tijuana cartel.

STEP ONE Situation Report (cont.)

Mexican Peso under seige	Mexican President tentative on IMF proposal; Mexican media claim the proposal is a scheme to control Mexican economy
IMF proposes emergency Mexican moves to better regulate Cyberpayments system	Florida bank arrests in Smart Card-based money laundering; front company tied to Tijuana cartel

In New York

On March 22, a nationally known **trader in international stock funds warned** that because of the continued social and economic instability **Mexico may soon have to be put on the "economic danger list."** Within an hour the **value of the Peso had fallen 10%** against the U.S. Dollar. Several mutual funds specializing in Mexican and Latin American stocks began to suffer from "panic selling."

In Washington

On March 24, the President of the **IMF** identified **money laundering** as the **major source of Mexico's Peso instability problem** and the major impediment to financial reform in Mexico. He announced a **draft IMF-led plan to bolster the Mexican economy, contingent on Mexico passing an array of executive orders and legislation** which would bring the Mexican cyberpayment system up to the U.S. and E.U. standards for currency security and anti-money laundering practices.

In Mexico City

On March 26, the President of Mexico told the U.S. Ambassador that Mexico **could "in principle" accept the IMF proposal** but that **"at least a month" would be needed to study the proposed legislation package**. That evening, several **major Mexican** TV news programs **attacked the IMF proposal** as serving the interests of American and European bankers who wanted to "take over the Mexican economy."

In West Palm Beach

On March 30, the **President of the *Southern Palms Bank*** was arrested and **charged with money laundering**. Advanced wiretap and Artificial Intelligence (AI) techniques had uncovered an **elaborate money laundering scheme exploiting several Smart Card systems**. The previously unseen *modus operandi* also employed advanced encryption methods and mobile satellite communications links to **transfer cash value to a variety of**

off-shore accounts, and communicate with a front company in Phoenix with **known connections to the Tijuana Cartel.**

"Walk-in" to the FBI reveals secret virus in ULTRA card; might be used for corrupting cards

GTO/NTO for San Diego and Phoenix regions to ascertain degree of Cyberpayment money laundering

Evidence found of Mexican bank involved in Cyberpayment system misuse

In San Francisco

On April 2, a "walk-in" to the FBI's San Francisco field office, a **senior computer programmer** employed by the ***SNYLOGIC* Corporation** (the developer of a highly popular and successful *ULTRA* stored value-type Smart Card) revealed that several months earlier he had found an **"unexplained virus" embedded in one of the key purse integrity elements of the *ULTRA* card.** He claimed he had not revealed his detection of this "anomaly" since he worried that his superiors had placed this "defect" for some classified corporate objective. His concern had been heightened after seeing Internet news reports about the Miami arrest of drug couriers with "corrupted" Smart Cards.

In Washington

In early May the Washington Post reported that on-going **analysis of the records of the *Southern Palms Bank*** in Coral Gables, Florida revealed **strong evidence** that a **major Mexico City bank** was in effect **under the control of the Guadalajara Cartel** and deeply involved in fraudulent activities that were contributing to **undermining the security of the Mexican Cyberpayments system.**

In San Diego and Phoenix

On May 15, at the request of the Financial Crime Coordination Council (FCCC), FinCEN initiated a **Geographic Targeting Order (GTO)** in the **San Diego and Phoenix regions** plus a **Network Targeting Order (NTO)** focused on suspected Cyberpayment money launderers.

The GTO/NTO combination was expected to induce sufficient effects to permit new FinCEN **Cyberpayment Artificial Intelligence (AI) routines** to **monitor any shifts to Cyberpayment money laundering techniques** as well as **identify previously unknown participants in money laundering operations.**

STEP ONE Situation Report (cont.)

Bitter partisan debate in the U.S. on how best to approach the escalating Mexican crisis	Mexican government politically paralyzed; Tijuana Cartel seeking deal contingent on gov't rejection of IMF proposal
U.S. NGOs organizing opposition to U.S. support for Mexican gov't	Intercept reveals ambiguous Guadalajara/ Cali anti-gov't "FIRE GOD" operation

In the United States

In late May a **bitter partisan fight on Mexican policy** broke out **in the U.S. Congress**. Opposition House and Senate members from California, Arizona, Texas, and Florida strongly attacked the President's "laissez-faire policy" and called for **military intervention against the drug cartels on the side of the Mexican government.** Prominent members from the Northeast and Northwest strongly supported the President and his strategy following the lines of the IMF proposal.

Several powerful non-governmental organizations (NGOs) including the "Free Mexico Movement" began organizing via the **Internet** calling for **opposition to any Administration action to "prop up a failed Mexican elite."**

In Mexico City

The absence of any Mexican legislative action on the IMF proposal continued to give the impression that **the Mexican Government was politically paralyzed.** High level rumors continued to claim that the **Tijuana Cartel** was **attempting to negotiate a formal "peace treaty"** with the Mexican government but insisting as the price of its support that the President **reject the IMF's proposed Cyberpayment modernization plan.**

In Guadalajara

On June 4, the U.S. was able to **break one of the Guadalajara Cartel's encrypted communication links** to its Cali allies. One message revealed a **previously unknown negotiating history** between the Guadalajara Cartel and a faction within the Mexican government. The message expressed alarm about the near success of the Tijuana Cartel's negotiations with the Mexican government and concluded that **"Operation FIRE GOD" should be launched "as soon as possible."** None of the decrypted messages **provided any concrete information on the character of Operation FIRE GOD.**

STEP ONE Situation Report (cont.)

London financiers arrested in plot to suborn Internet service provider for money laundering

Swiss HUMINT indicates Guadalajara/Cali economic destabilization plan - seeking to effect removal of current Mexican President

U.S. fails to get Mexican government to close Mexico City bank involved in Cyberpayment misuse

In London

On June 30 the Metropolitan Police Department's Fraud Squad announced the **arrest of six prominent Bond Street financiers** in connection with an alleged **drug cartel money laundering operation.** The brokers had **planned to take control of the U.K.'s third largest Internet service provider** which was to become an integral part of a new money laundering operation **to replace the Cali Cartel's primary European money laundering infrastructure** and its historical reliance on currency smuggling and the international wire transfer system.

In Switzerland

On July 4th, an **urgent message** from the Office of the Federal Chancellor of Switzerland to the U.S. National Security Advisor warned of **"human intelligence" via** connections in the Swiss banking system indicating that the **Guadalajara and Cali Cartels** were planning an **"economic destabilization plan"** aimed at **"removing and replacing" the current Mexican Government and his political allies in the reform movement.** The plan was reported to include efforts to manipulate the Mexican **stock market,** the Mexican **national Cyberpayment system**, and the **value of the Peso** on world currency markets.

Cartel funds obtained in the destabilization operation and other **Cartel funds** now in Mexican banks were to be **transferred as soon as possible to European and Asian financial institutions** in anticipation of severe Mexican economic instabilities.

In Washington

On July 9th, the Washington Post reported that **U.S. authorities** had been **unsuccessful in persuading the Mexican government to close immediately the Mexico City bank** that was involved with the Coral Gables *Southern Palms Bank* in fraudulent Cyberpayment-related activities. The article cited this situation as **"evidence of the inadequacy of Mexican Cyberpayment policing."**

Moscow meeting of Cali Cartel and Russian mafiya reps on Smart Card-based money laundering scheme	Joint NSC/NEC meeting called to address escalating Mexican crisis
Florida DEA-led operation reveals evidence of transfer of $100 million from Guadalajara Cartel to political adversaries of Mexican President	Treasury and Justice asked to prepare issues (and any recommendations) for NSC/NEC meeting on key "near-term tactical and longer-term strategic" Cyberpayment misuse issues

In Moscow

On July 8th U.S. intelligence sources reported that **Cali Cartel** representatives had recently finalized the **procedures for a new money laundering operation**: The Colombians would **deliver U.S. Dollars to a mafiya-controlled Russian bank** for which they would **receive bulk packages of $100 Smart Cards.** The **Smart Cards** would be **express mailed to a bank in Yakutsk** and deposited in the account of **a Russian/Colombian joint venture mining company.** The **funds** would then be **wire transferred to a bank in St. Petersburg** and then on **to the Swiss account of a cartel front company** ostensibly involved in international mining.

In Panama City, Florida

On July 14, a DEA-led operation resulted in the **capture of a major Guadalajara Cartel "safe house" and communications center**. Examination of weakly encrypted computer records found at the site revealed **evidence of a transfer of funds - estimated at over $200 million - to various individuals and enterprises to buy** political support within disaffected elements in the Mexican government.

In Washington

On July 15 the President asked for an immediate **joint meeting** of the **National Security Council** and **National Economic Council** to: (1) **discuss the escalating Mexican crisis** and **(2) take this opportunity to also discuss the "full range of tactical and strategic Cyberpayment misuse issues."**

As part of the preparations for that meeting, the Secretary of the Treasury and the Attorney General were asked to prepare a set of **recommendations** on the **key "near-**

term tactical and longer-term strategic" Cyberpayment-related issues that they believe need to be decided at this time.

STEP ONE
Instructions

How to Proceed

1. You will have a total of **60 minutes** to complete your deliberations on STEP ONE.

2. You are in the role of a member of the **Financial Crimes Coordination Council (FCCC)** which is chaired by the Under Secretary of the Treasury (Enforcement) and the Deputy Attorney General and reports to the Secretary of the Treasury and the Attorney General.

3. You are in a group deliberative and drafting process **finalizing a Draft Memo** for the Secretary of the Treasury and the Attorney General in advance of a combined National Security Council (NSC)/National Economic Council (NEC) meeting with the President on the Mexican financial crisis and other Cyberpayment-related issues.

4. At that NSC/NEC meeting the Secretary of the Treasury and Attorney General will present:

- The key tactical and strategic Cyberpayment-related **issues** that Treasury and Justice believe should be decided at this time and

- Treasury and Justice's **recommendations** on those issues.

5. The **Chair of the group** will lead a discussion that moves through the tasking described in the Decisions to Be Made section in the column to the right.

6. The Chair will begin by asking each of the **participants** to **very briefly give their individual perspectives** - their "take" - on the key facets and overall character of the situation presented.

7. The Chair will ask one of the participants to record the group's changes to the Draft Memo and group recommendations on specific issues.

8. NOTE: The Chair of each group will be asked to summarize the group's deliberations and recommendations on STEP ONE (and STEP TWO) at the end of STEP TWO (see Agenda).

Decisions to Be Made

I. Issues and Options

Several members of the Financial Crimes Coordination Council (FCCC) met earlier and prepared the **"issues and options" Draft Memo** on the following pages. This Draft Memo provides an initial cut at what might go forward to the Secretary of the Treasury and the Attorney General on a proposed set of near-term tactical and longer-term strategic Cyberpayment-related issues and the evolving situation in Mexico.

Under the guidance of the Chair, the group should **expand and modify the Draft Memo as judged appropriate** in the light of the situation. If there are issues or options beyond those presented which the group thinks should be addressed at this point in time, it should modify the Draft Memo accordingly.

2. Recommendations

Over the course of discussing and settling on the issues and options to go forward to the Secretary of the Treasury and the Attorney General, the Chair will undertake to **see if the group can reach consensus on recommendations** on individual issues.

If there is **a strong and unreconcilable divergence of views on some issue**, the Chair will conduct a **vote on the options** still on the table and record the vote for communication to the Secretary of the Treasury and the Attorney General.

Keep in mind that at this point a consensus on all issues - and especially on the most difficult and divisive issues - is not necessarily expected.

STEP ONE
DRAFT MEMO

Department of the Treasury

15 July 2004

MEMORANDUM FOR THE SECRETARY OF THE TREASURY
THE ATTORNEY GENERAL

FROM: Under Secretary (Enforcement)
Deputy Attorney General

SUBJECT: Cyberpayment System Misuse and the Mexican Crisis

Per your request, below you will find a set of candidate near-term tactical and longer-term strategic issues relating to Cyberpayment system misuse for possible presentation to the President at tomorrow's joint NSC/NEC meeting.

The issues presented reflect a consensus within the Financial Crimes Coordination Council (FCCC) as to the issues of this nature that the U.S. Government needs to address at this time in order to:

1. better enable law enforcement to check the further spread of Cyberpayment-related money laundering;
2. better secure U.S. Cyberpayment systems and the U.S. Cyberpayment system users in the larger global Cyberpayment environment;

BACKGROUND

Evidence from recent investigations indicates that certain types of Cyberpayment products are increasingly being used within the U.S. and elsewhere to launder funds from drug trafficking operations and other illegal activities.

At the same time that this "Cyber-laundering" is on the rise, FCCC member agencies are reporting that conventional investigative methods and resources are increasingly ineffective against these new payment system technologies.

This problem has become particularly acute with respect to Mexico. As currently configured, Mexico's Cyberpayment regulatory and law enforcement oversight procedures are primitive even by current (modest) U.S. and E.U. standards – and as such are being exploited in money laundering activities by Mexican drug cartels. If

left unchecked, these weaknesses may undermine the much stronger protective measures that we are now trying to implement here in the U.S. and elsewhere. The precedent of Antigua emphasizes that Cyberpayment system abuse can undermine national economic viability.
Recent intelligence indicates that Colombian and Mexican drug cartels are pooling their funds within the Mexican Cyberpayment system prior to their transfer into the U.S. The volume of these funds, and the involvement of significant Mexican banking institutions in their transmittal, has features that are beginning to resemble the slow corruption process that took shape in the 1990s in Colombia. As in Colombia, evidence has appeared that Mexican drug cartel principals are purchasing controlling interests in leading infrastructure sectors within the Mexican economy. Over the long term this presents a potential pressure point that drug cartels may use to impede law enforcement efforts by the Mexican government.

At this time, working through the IMF, we are attempting to remedy the deteriorating situation in Mexico through immediate Mexican agreement and action on much needed Cyberpayment system oversight legislation. With this legislation in hand, Mexican law enforcement authorities will be in a much better position to combat Cyberpayment system abuse and successfully prosecute drug cartel principals.

We have formulated the issues and possible responses to the Cyberpayment system security challenge in terms of both near-term tactical and longer-term strategic questions. Beyond the requirements of immediate crisis management, there is clearly an opportunity in the current environment to address broad Cyberpayment system oversight concerns and means by which to positively influence the overall global Cyberpayment system environment.

TACTICAL ISSUES

The recent experience in the Phoenix and San Diego areas of coordinating a more traditional Geographic Targeting Order (GTO) with a Cyberpayment Network Targeting Order (CNTO) proved moderately successful. The GTO/CNTO combination appears to offer a relatively unobtrusive and low cost way of gaining important information of utility to law enforcement and Cyberpayment system regulators, to include insights into the practices and patterns of misuse of Cyberpayment networks by suspected money launderers. At present, it is estimated that fully 15 per cent of all of the funds transferred through Cyberpayment systems derive from illicit purposes such as money laundering. This level of fraud and abuse cannot be tolerated over an extended period without highly negative consequences relating to the credibility and integrity of the Cyberpayment infrastructure as a whole.

In the light of current circumstances, more ambitious GTO/CNTO combinations might be launched in a larger number of "high priority" cities where the Guadalajara and Tijuana cartels are known to operate (as well as returning to Phoenix and San Diego) as a means of gaining a more systematic understanding of current patterns of Cyberpayment abuse in the United States.

While most Cyberpayment instrument users accept the need for issuers to electronically monitor Cyberpayment systems to combat fraud and comparable problems, there remain questions as to just what the level of intrusion for broader law enforcement purposes will be judged acceptable in light of Constitutional and privacy concerns.

The tactical issues that need to be addressed at this time would appear to be:

1. Should coordinated GTOs and CNTOs be put into effect in U.S. cities where drug traffickers working with the Mexican cartels are believed to be operating?

   _____A. Yes. The Integrated GTO/CNTO program should target:

   _____i. All of the designated "high priority" cities (Atlanta, Dallas, El Paso, Houston, Los Angeles, Miami, Phoenix, and San Diego)

   _____ii. A smaller set of cities: ______________________________

   _____iii. ______________________________

   _____B. No. Not at this time.

2. (If the answer to Question #1 is Yes) Against what target sets should the CNTO measures be implemented?

   _____A. Stored value-type Smart Cards and e-cash systems used by merchants suspected of involvement in money laundering.

   _____B. Stored value-type Smart Cards issued by U.S. Cyberpayment companies that have been used by foreign nationals in the preceding 60-day period.

   _____C. A "blanket" capture and analysis of targeted data for all merchant and consumer stored-value payment instruments that meet certain criteria used in the targeted cities for a fixed period, namely ____________.

   _____D. ______________________________.

   _____E. ______________________________.

3. Should the U.S. seek to launch an immediate study by key G-7/FATF members on patterns in the abuse of Cyberpayment systems to determine whether Transnational Criminal Organizations (TCOs) are coordinating the manipulation of Cyberpayment systems throughout the world?

   _____A. Yes. Focus on investigating the activities of:

_____ i. The international drug cartels.

_____ ii. ______________________________.

_____B. No. The U.S. should complete its own national Cyberpayment system security study before it proposes a global investigation to its G-7/FATF partners.

STRATEGIC ISSUES

MEASURING THE EFFECTIVENESS OF ANTI-MONEY LAUNDERING EFFORTS

Traditional law enforcement tools and techniques for combating money laundering may be in the process of being undermined by the emergence of Cyberpayment systems. In this evolving context, evaluating both existing techniques for combating money laundering and proposed new techniques such as CNTOs becomes increasingly important. This raises the prospect of attempting to establish broadly accepted measures of effectiveness (MOEs) to apply to the various efforts to combat money laundering – recognizing that quantitative measures of effectiveness in law enforcement are inherently very difficult to achieve.

1. Should additional effort be directed to the development of new and improved MOEs for anti-money laundering tools and techniques?

_____A. Yes. The MOEs that warrant examination include:

_____i. The price paid for the laundering of illicit funds.

_____ ii. The magnitude and proportionality of funds laundered through Cyberpayment systems versus other techniques.

_____ iii. The sensitivity of money laundering behavior to the imposition of GTO/CNTO-type investigative techniques.

_____ iv. The potential deterrent significance of coordinated CNTOs and GTOs in countering money laundering and drug trafficking.

_____v. ______________________________________.

_____ vi. ______________________________________.

_____B. No. Not at this time.

AFFECTING STORED VALUE-TYPE SMART CARD FUNCTIONALITY

The accessibility measures designed by issuers to gather information on Cyberpayment instrument use for management purposes (and exploited by CNTOs) could also be employed to alter the functionality (ceiling, expiration date, etc.) of deployed Cyberpayment instruments.

In light of this situation law enforcement authorities might be given the authority to compel issuers to terminate or restrict the functionality of stored value-type Smart Cards in selected circumstances, e.g., when card use meets a well understood profile of illicit activity. Perhaps not surprisingly, the ACLU and other civil liberties advocates have already addressed this prospect as representing an unjustified trend toward the expansion of law enforcement powers over Cyberpayment system operators.

1. Should the further investigation of network-based investigative methods include the possibility of compelling issuers to terminate or otherwise restrict the functionality of stored value-type Smart Cards?

_____A. Yes.

_____B. No. Such measures may violate public views regarding individual privacy.

_____C. Other Response.

____

____

FinCEN

Cyberpayment Systems Exercise

Tab I

STEP TWO

RAND

2 June 1997

Tab I
STEP TWO Situation Report

In Washington

At and after the July 16 NSC/NEC meeting, the **President** made **the following decisions:**

- Initiate **NTOs AND GTOs in designated high priority cities**.

- Limit **NTOs** to those **Cyberpayment instruments held by known or suspected money launderers** or **drug cartel-related entities.**

- Initiate discussions within the **G-7/FATF** framework on a possible **study of patterned abuse in global Cyberpayment systems**.

- **Undertake** an immediate **study** of potential **anti-money laundering measures of effectiveness**; an **initial objective** will be **determining** the internal U.S. and international variations in the **price paid by drug traffickers for money laundering.**

- **Postpone further government investigation** of the possibility of **manipulating Smart Card functionality**.

- **Delay** any discussions of a **joint U.S.-Mexican Cyberpayment System Oversight Facility** pending **the outcome** of the current Mexican financial crisis.

In Washington

On July 18, after a review by the **National Security Agency**, the newly modified **encryption software** for SYNLOGIC's **Smart Card *ULTRA*** which **(in wide use in Mexico as well as in the U.S.)** was declared **"secure."**

In Atlanta

In an apparent **response to the GTO declared for the Atlanta area**, money transmitters subject to increased surveillance appeared to be suffering a loss of business. A **surge in the use of Cyberpayment systems** by suspected money launderers was detected, however, in both **Phoenix and Chicago**.

In Mexico City

On July 20, a **senior Mexican Justice Department official**, a **close political ally of the President**, was **killed** during a **wild shoot-out** between his attackers and Federal Police bodyguards. Rumors throughout the Mexican political elite and media strongly pointed to **opponents of the President and his crackdown on the Guadalajara and Cali Cartels.**

During a **multi-media address** that evening, the **Mexican President voiced defiance** and a continued "commitment to root out the cancer which grips Mexican society." He announced that he was convening a **special session of the Mexican Congress** three days hence **to seek formal endorsement of the IMF economic stabilization and assistance proposal** and **enact the associated regulatory and law enforcement legislation.**

On July 26th, after a stormy and protracted debate, a strong majority of the **Mexican Congress endorsed the IMF proposal** and **passed an initial set of Cyberpayment regulatory and law enforcement statutes in what was labeled the "Mexican Financial Security Act of 2002."** Media commentators in Mexico, the U.S., and Canada hailed this **"act of political courage and decisiveness by the Mexican President."**

In San Francisco

On July 27, the ***SYNLOGIC*** "whistle blower" **programmer** went public on CNN with accusations that the **security in the new encryption scheme** in the ***ULTRA*** **Smart Cards** was **still flawed -** claiming **government "cover-up or incompetence."**

In Washington

On July 30th, the President of Mexico was received at the White House by the U.S. President and the Presidents of the IMF and European Union. That afternoon, an agreement implementing the **IMF's economic stabilization plan for Mexico was signed at a White House ceremony.**

During a series of background meetings with the media, the National Security Advisor and Secretary of Treasury revealed that a U.S. assistance package was going to Mexico to provide **"emergency technological and equipment support" to the Mexican Army and Federal Police.** The support included the increased use of

American surveillance platforms to assist Mexican counter-insurgency operations in southern Mexico.

In Canada

The **campaign to "roll-up" the Guadalajara money laundering structure** in the U.S. and Canada continued to yield **new successes** - aided by a **continuing flow of information from the Tijuana Cartel to Mexican authorities**. One of the most dramatic incidents in the widely-covered effort was the early August **suicide of the vice president for international currency trading of a major bank in Toronto** which had been compromised by **"Operation CLEAN SWEEP."**

In Mexico

As part of the implementation of the "Mexican Financial Security Act of 2002," **banks, Cyberpayment issuers, and money transmitters operating in Mexico** were required "for six months" to **certify that customers using Cyberpayment instruments of any kind were legal "persons" and not named on a long list of individuals** known to be **connected with money laundering activities** (assembled by Mexican law enforcement officials and payment system regulators, aided by their U.S. counterparts).

In Tijuana

On August 4th in Tijuana, a **Cyberpayment issuer** that was unable to certify the identities of a large number of stored value payment instrument holders was **closed by the Mexican Government**. This was the **first enforcement of institutional seizure provisions** of the Mexican Financial Security Act of 2002.

In Colon, Panama

On August 7th after considerable pressure by the U.S., the Panamanian President ordered the seizure, with the cooperation of the US military units, of the ***Southern Star,* a Liberian-registered vessel. The cargo that was seized which included a huge cache of advanced infantry weapons, including surface-to-air missiles and night combat equipment, a significant quantity of cocaine, and $200 million in US currency.** Evidence found on board the ship suggested that the crew of the *Southern Star* picked up the arms cargo at Port Haracourt, Nigeria from a Serbian source.

In Monterey

During a clandestine meeting with **U.S. Chief of Station and the head of DEA** operations in Mexico, the **Chief of Staff of the Federal Police** provided detailed targeting information on the structure of the **Guadalajara Cartel's most sophisticated money laundering operations** in the **midwest and southeast regions of the United States.** This information was immediately transmitted to the Directors of the FBI, FinCEN, and the chairperson of the Financial Crimes Coordination Council (FCCC).

In Mexico City

On August 14th, the **President of Mexico** during his weekly "war council" with his most trusted members of the government ordered the launching of an all-out effort to **prosecute and arrest the Guadalajara Cartel by arresting and prosecuting its leaders.**

That evening, the **U.S. Ambassador** received a **"disturbing" report** from a senior member of the Mexican government that a **"peace treaty" with the Tijuana Cartel would be offered to the Mexican Government within a "matter of days."**

In Rural Mexico

A **particularly unpopular element** of the financial reforms among rural groups in Mexico was the requirement that **individuals submit identification records** to receive **new stored value-type Smart Cards.** This measure was **widely viewed** as **an attempt** by the Mexican government **to identify local community leaders** and to **seize funds controlled by political opponents.**

In late August the **Mexican government** implemented a Cyberpayment **data collection effort** akin to a U.S. **Network Targeting Order (NTO)** in Guadalajara, Monterey, and Juarez. As part of the **procedure, all users of** Cyberpayment instruments were subject to scrutiny according to their **owner's identities**, the **initial source of deposited funds**, and **recent transactions.**

As a result of this information collection effort, it was discovered that **many stored value cards** in Mexico were **issued in the names of deceased individuals.** In addition, many **stored value e-cash accounts** were found to be under the control of known **insurgent and drug trafficking entities.**

In Washington

During an emergency **meeting of the FCCC**, the **Deputy Director of NSA** provided evidence indicating that the **Guadalajara and Cali Cartels** had "probably" **ordered the execution of the still not fully understood Operation FIRE GOD.** It was increasingly clear, however, that the principal **objective of FIRE GOD was to replace the existing Mexican Government with a "less hostile" administrations at both the national and state levels**. A State Department representative at the meeting confirmed that "some kind of **anti-government political operation had been launched in Mexico City.**"

After a several hour discussion of the evidence, the FCCC drafted a memorandum to the Secretary of Treasury and the Attorney General indicating that **the Cali and Guadalajara Cartels** appeared to have "embarked upon a **major economic and political destabilization campaign against the Mexican President and his allies** based in part on **manipulation of the Mexican Cyberpayments system.**"

The Day After

In Monterey

On September 22, several major **Mexican and U.S. banks detected a massive outflow of currency** from Mexico. By that afternoon, the **Mexican stock exchange had suspended trading after a collapse of value in excess of 8%.** In turn, the value of the **Peso fell by nearly 10%** before a **massive intervention by the Mexican central bank.**

In Washington

During a **National Security Council meeting**, the Secretary of Treasury announced that **the Mexican Government** was **"showing signs of panic" on the country's financial situation** and was prepared to **"radically restrict the flow of currency out of Mexico including draconian restrictions on Cyberpayment transfers."**

The Secretary also noted that the FCCC assessment indicated that the **Cali Cartel's Operation FIRE GOD included a massive effort to flood the Mexican economy with counterfeit e-money as part of an** effort to **subvert** the **Cyberpayment system.**

In Mexico City

At 1300 local time, September 26, the **Mexican government declared a "bank holiday" and "temporarily" closed Mexico City's Bolsa stock exchange.** Early indications from U.S. banking sources indicated that the **Mexican government's effort to staunch the "hemorrhage" of currency out of Mexico was failing.**

In Washington

A **joint meeting of the National Security Council and National Economic Council** was called for September 28th to discuss **the escalating Mexican crisis** and **the possibility of the U.S. undertaking "new and urgent measures"** to thwart the Cali and Guadalajara Cartels' ongoing destabilization campaign against the Mexican President and his administration.

As part of the preparations for the meeting the National Security Advisor asked the Secretary of the Treasury and the Attorney General to prepare a set of **recommendations** on the **Cyberpayment-related issues** that they believed needed to be addressed in the context of the ongoing Mexican Government.

STEP TWO INSTRUCTIONS

How to Proceed

1. You will have a total of **60 minutes** to complete your reading and deliberations on STEP TWO.

2. Your instructions are essentially the same as in STEP ONE.

3. You are again in the role of a member of the **Financial Crimes Coordination Council (FCCC)** - chaired by the Under Secretary of the Treasury (Enforcement) and the Deputy Attorney General and **reporting to the Secretary of the Treasury and the Attorney General.**

4. You are again in a group deliberative and drafting process. In this case your are finalizing a **Memo from the Secretary of the Treasury and the Attorney General to the President** in advance of a joint NSC/NEC on the Mexican crisis.

5. The Chair of your group will again lead a discussion that moves through the tasking described in the Decisions to Be Made section in the column to the right.

6. <u>NOTE</u>: The Chair of each group will be asked to summarize the group's deliberations and recommendations on STEP TWO (and STEP ONE) at the end of STEP TWO (see Agenda).

Decisions to Be Made

I. Issues and Options

Under the guidance of the Chair, the group should **expand and modify the Draft Memo** as judged appropriate in the light of the situation.

2. Recommendations

The Chair will again undertake to **see if the group can reach consensus on recommendations** on individual issues.

STEP TWO: The Day After ... Draft Memo for the President

The White House

27 September 2004

MEMORANDUM FOR THE PRESIDENT

FROM: The Secretary of the Treasury
The Attorney General

SUBJECT: Cyberpayment Issues Relating to the Mexican Crisis

As requested, this memorandum lays out a set of key Cyberpayment-related issues for consideration at the 9:00 am NSC/NEC meeting on the Mexican political and financial crisis.

We understand that that meeting will address both the ongoing destabilization campaign by the Cali and Guadalajara Drug Cartels aimed at the Mexican Government and possible near-term measures for enhancing the security of the U.S. and Mexican Cyberpayment infrastructures.

OBJECTIVES

We would appear to have the following Cyberpayment related objectives in this evolving situation:

- Protect the integrity of the U.S. Cyberpayment system and protect U.S. Cyberpayment users from spillover damage caused by the Mexican financial crisis;
- Take short term measures responding to the security problems recently revealed in the U.S. and Mexican Cyberpayment systems;
- Take advantage of the Mexican situation to stimulate action within the broader international financial community to improve overall Cyberpayment system security.

The issues presented on the following pages are intended to be seen as the Cyberpayment elements of a larger action plan that would serve to thwart the Guadalajara and Cali Cartels' destabilization campaign.

FOLLOW UP ACTIONS FROM THE MULTI-CITY CNTO

The recent CNTOs demonstrate the advantages of selective targeting of stored value-type Smart Cards and other financial resources held by suspected money launderers.

At this time, the U.S. may wish to seek curtailment of the functionality of some of the Smart Cards identified in the CNTOs (in addition to seizing the assets in money laundering accounts and banks and regulated financial institutions) as a way to protect the credibility and integrity of the U.S. Cyberpayment infrastructure. On the other hand, such action might be taken only after a thorough examination of the implications of such an order for the U.S. Cyberpayment system as a whole.

The CNTO also identified Cyberpayment issuers associated with drug-related money laundering. In defense of the U.S. Cyberpayment system, consideration could be given to the closure of U.S. financial institutions deemed to be suborned by drug cartels.

The near term issues that need to be addressed at this time are:

1. Should the U.S. urgently compel Cyberpayment instrument issuers to suspend the functionality of stored value-type Smart Cards held by merchants suspected of money laundering activities?

    ______A. Yes.

    ______B. Not yet but probably; first immediately initiate a thorough review of the impact on the overall payment system of the proposed actions;

    ______C. No. This kind of action is unwarranted at this time.

2. What actions should the U.S. Government take against Cyberpayment issuers whose stored value-type Smart Cards are suspected of being used for money laundering?

    ______A. Place such institutions under governmental administrative control pending the outcome of criminal prosecutions.

    ______B. Issue Investigative Advisory Notices (formal warnings) to these Cyberpayment issuers with the simultaneous imposition of a targeted CNTO to build an evidentiary base for further investigations and possible prosecution.

    ______C. Issue Investigative Advisory Notices to these Cyberpayment issuers.

    ______D. ____.

_____E. Take no action at this time.

NETWORK INVESTIGATION AND LAW ENFORCEMENT

The use of GTOs and CNTOs has added importantly to the law enforcement community's understanding of the scope of drug cartel activities across the United States. It is particularly apparent, for instance, that drug cartels are actively seeking to exploit Cyberpayment systems for money laundering purposes.

In the light of this information, an expansion in the coverage of GTO/CNTO investigations to a larger number of US cities may be advisable to help produce a baseline for future targeted investigations of fraud and abuse in Cyberpayment networks.

Recent public disclosures of the possible compromise of security in the popular Smart Card ULTRA system have raised a new set of questions about the integrity of both the U.S. and Mexican Cyberpayment infrastructures. In this situation it may be wise to set the precedent of conducting a thorough government security review of the ULTRA card and any other suspect Cyberpayment instruments.

1. Should the use of coordinated GTO/CNTOs be significantly expanded to other U.S. cities to evaluate broader patterns of abuse in Cyberpayment systems in the U.S.?

    _____A. Yes.

    _____B. No. Not at this time.

2. Should an immediate review of the security of the ULTRA stored value-type Smart Card system, and any other suspect Cyberpayment instruments, be conducted by the Government?

    _____A. Yes, and the review should be a joint government-industry effort involving Smart Card and other Cyberpayment instrument manufacturers.

    _____B. No. Not at this time.

ASSISTANCE TO THE MEXICAN CYBERPAYMENT SYSTEM

A significant modernization of the Mexican Cyberpayment system would provide the Mexican Government with powerful new tools to combat widespread criminal activity and money laundering.

Because of the importance of ongoing efforts by the current Mexican administration toward such modernization, we may wish to take direct action to further assist Mexican authorities in identifying instances of fraud and abuse within the Mexican Cyberpayment infrastructure. In particular, we might show them how to carry out more effective computer-based investigations into Cyberpayment system security.

The issue that needs addressing in this category is:

1. Should the United States offer to assist Mexico in conducting CNTO-like investigations of the Mexican Cyberpayment infrastructure?

   _____A. Yes, but with the following restrictions:

   _____ i. Any CNTO-related tools and techniques should be utilized under the control of U.S. personnel, with only broad surveillance information being shared with Mexican law enforcement personnel.

   _____ ii. ____.

   _____ iii. ____.

   _____B. No. CNTO-related investigative techniques should not be shared with Mexico under any circumstances.

INTERNATIONAL COLLABORATION

The broader implications of a Mexican Cyberpayment system collapse warrant the utilization of international policy coordination mechanisms to help bring Cyberpayment systems under more effective governmental control.

The interconnection of national Cyberpayment infrastructures opens the possibility that a collapse in one location could destabilize economies and Cyberpayment systems elsewhere. As a precautionary measure to guard against such an eventuality:

1. Should the U.S. seek immediate G-7/FATF assistance in coordinating an international response to the apparent drug cartel suborning of the Mexican Cyberpayment system?

   _____A. Yes. Discussions should be initiated immediately.

   _____B. No. The International Monetary Fund Assistance Package and established patterns of ad hoc policy coordination are a sufficient response to the crisis.

   _____C. Other Response: ____

2. Should the United States launch a series of bilateral and multilateral initiatives to find and initiate legal proceedings against any Cyberpayment issuers believed to have been suborned by the Cali, Guadalajara or Tijuana Cartels?

_____A. Yes.

_____B. Not at this time. Such initiatives require that considerable evidence be gathered prior to action. Insufficient investigative background work has been done to support such an effort.

_____C. No. The United States possesses its own information and investigative resources. It should proceed when it feels it necessary, conducting unilateral action against suspected criminally suborned Cyberpayment issuers if necessary.

_____D. Other Response: ____

____

____

FinCEN

Cyberpayment Systems Exercise

Tab J

STEP THREE

2 June 1997

RAND

TAB J
STEP THREE INSTRUCTIONS

How to Proceed

1. You will have a total of **80 minutes** to complete your reading and deliberations on STEP THREE.

2. **First read the next page.** It summarizes some of the key regulatory and law enforcement issues generated by the emergence of Cyberpayment systems.

3. In this step you are now back in the relative near future - to be precise in July of 1998.

4. You are in the role of a member of the **Interagency Cyberpayment Study Group (ICSG),** an interagency study group made up of representatives from the financial regulatory and law enforcement communities.

5. The ICSG has been working under the direction of the **Electronic Commerce Security Committee (ECSC)** which was created in October 1997 to implement Presidential Review Directive/National Security Council 118 (PRD/NSC-118) which gave the ECSC a nine month charter to:

- Conduct a comprehensive examination of the vulnerability of Cyberpayment products to exploitation for money laundering and

- Assess existing potentially relevant regulatory and law enforcement regimes and make recommendations regarding appropriate Cyberpayment system oversight.

6. You are in a group deliberative and drafting process preparing the final draft of a Memo to the ECSC summarizing the principal issues and options that emerged from the PRD/NSC-118 study.

7. The Chair of your group will again lead a discussion that expands and modifies the Draft Memo as judged appropriate.

8. The Chair will again undertake to see if the group can reach consensus on recommendations on individual issues.

9. The Chair of each group will again be asked to summarize the group's deliberations and recommendations at the end of STEP THREE.

REGULATORY AND LAW ENFORCEMENT ISSUES GENERATED BY THE EMERGENCE OF CYBERPAYMENT SYSTEMS

The regulatory and law enforcement issues raised by the emergence of Cyberpayment systems can be examined within four basic categories: (1) Definitional Issues - those pertaining to the transactional nature of Cyberpayment instruments as vehicles for transferring value; (2) International coordination of regulatory oversight and law enforcement work relating to Cyberpayment systems; (3) Cyberpayment Regulatory Issues - deriving from the characteristics of the standards and technologies used in Cyberpayment systems; and (4) Law Enforcement Issues - relating to the investigative techniques and information-access issues raised by Cyberpayment systems.

A set of questions relating to each of these issue areas is given below to help focus the discussions during STEP THREE regarding Cyberpayment system oversight.

(1) Definitional Issues

The treatment of Cyberpayment instruments (Currency? Some other monetary instrument? Neither? Both) for the purposes of regulatory oversight and law enforcement anti-abuse investigations

(2) International Anti-Money Laundering Policy Coordination Issues

International oversight over globally deployed Cyberpayment systems

Coordinated enforcement of legal orders relating to Cyberpayment systems

Development of joint policies relating to non-FATF members with emerging Cyberpayment Infrastructures

(3) Regulatory Issues

Harmonization of oversight rules for Cyberpayment products

Harmonization of rules regarding the identities of permissible issuers of Cyberpayment products

The best regulatory approach for influencing the emergence of a safe and secure Cyberpayment infrastructure

(4) Law Enforcement Issues

Restrictions to be imposed on governmental access to Cyberpayment system records

Types of information derived from Cyberpayment systems that should be shared with International partners in programs for combating the corrupt use of electronic payment infrastructures

STEP THREE

DRAFT MEMO

Department of the Treasury

XX July 1998

MEMORANDUM TO: Electronic Commerce Security Committee (ECSC)

FROM: Executive Director – Interagency Cyberpayment Study Group (ICSG)

SUBJECT: Report on Cyberpayment System Vulnerability to Criminal Exploitation for Money Laundering

As you are aware, the anticipated problem of criminal misuse of Cyberpayment systems prompted the President in October 1997 to issue Presidential Review Directive/National Security Council #118 (PRD/NSC-118). PRD/NSC-118 established the Electronic Commerce Security Committee (ECSC) and gave that committee a nine month charter to conduct a comprehensive examination of Cyberpayment products, focusing on their operational characteristics and vulnerability to criminal misuse. The ECSC was also instructed to assess existing regulatory and law enforcement regimes and make recommendations regarding Cyberpayment system oversight.

The Interagency Cyberpayment Study Group (ICSG), working under ECSC direction, has completed the review called for by PRD/NSC-118. The purpose of this memorandum is to summarize the findings and recommendations in that review.

OVERVIEW

There has been substantial speculation concerning the possible vulnerability of Cyberpayment systems to criminal misuse, particularly for money laundering. Law enforcement officials may find that for some Cyberpayment systems, existing regulations are not readily applicable and traditional investigative techniques are ineffective. As a consequence, it may become increasingly difficult in some instances to construct viable money laundering cases for prosecution.

The global nature of internationally operating Cyberpayment systems may also present many unique and difficult problems to both investigators and Cyberpayment system regulators. As such, international collaboration among like-minded countries (using the precedents set by the G-7/FATF and the G-10) is a critical part of effective Cyberpayment system oversight.

The work of the ICSG has also surfaced supervisory, consumer, and privacy issues that must be factored into the decision making process. Any attempt to develop effective techniques for surveillance and investigation in the Cyber-world must clearly comply with constitutional safeguards. Due consideration must also be given to the development of appropriate procedures for the maintenance and dissemination of information collected during criminal investigations.

In a similar vein, due consideration must be given to the impact of any new laws or regulations on the development of the Cyberpayments industry – including the impact of increased costs and decreased efficiency.

Near term decisions on Cyberpayment oversight will have considerable impact on the longer-term challenge of combating the potential misuse of Cyberpayment systems by money launderers. The security of the Cyberpayment infrastructure itself may be at risk if these challenges are not adequately addressed by public policy.

I. DEFINING THE NATURE OF CYBERPAYMENT VALUE

Cyberpayment value is in many respects similar to cash and other monetary instruments. However, these instruments differ from traditional currency in that they allow unprecedented speed in the transfer of value between consumers across global distances, and that they possess a considerable potential for transactor anonymity.

From the vantage point of payment system oversight, the exact nature of Cyberpayment value, and of the appropriate regulatory treatment for it, is a subject that remains unresolved. A key question concerns the applicability of the Bank Secrecy Act (BSA) (summarized in the Appendix to Tab C) to Cyberpayment value.

1. Should Cyberpayment value be subject to the Bank Secrecy Act for the purposes of regulatory and law enforcement oversight?

______A. Yes.

______B. Yes, but anticipate revisiting this issue when the Cyberpayment industry and market place are further developed.

______C. No. Judge each Cyberpayment instrument separately as to whether it should be covered by the BSA or some other legislation and regulations.

______D. No. Treat Cyberpayments as an entirely new form of value transfer vehicle that requires entirely new regulatory and law enforcement treatment.

______E. Other Response: ____

____

____

II. CYBERPAYMENT SYSTEM ISSUES

Effective oversight of Cyberpayment systems will require close collaboration between Cyberpayment network operators and governmental regulators. Public-private cooperation could extend from the sharing of information all the way to government mandates on the identity of permissible Cyberpayment value issuers and the functionality permitted for Cyberpayment products.

The issues that need to be addressed in this category are:

1. Should U.S. Government oversight of the Cyberpayment industry be based principally on collaborative public-private management of a regime defining permissible categories of:

    _____A. Functionality

    _____B. Types of Issuers

    _____C. Other Criteria: ______________________________

    ____

    ____

2. (If the answer to the above question is " A. Functionality", what types of functionality should be subject to regulation?

    _____A. Size and frequency of peer-to-peer value transfers

    _____B. Application Longevity

    _____C. Transaction Records

    _____D. Card Denomination Limits

    _____E. Frequency of Permissible Transactions

    _____F. Other Criteria: ______________________________

____

____

3. (If the answer to the above question is "B. Issuers") What types of businesses should be permitted to issue Cyberpayment value?

_____A. Banks.

_____B. Non-Bank Financial Institutions

_____C. Telecommunications System Operators or

_____D. Computer Software Firms

_____E. Any business that agrees to operate under the Bank Secrecy Act and other applicable regulations (some yet to be developed)

_____F. Other Criteria: ______________________________

____

____

4. Should the U.S. consider developing a value-tagging system to track transfer of electronic value?

_____A. Yes. Such a system should be developed by:

_____i. The Government

_____ ii. Private Industry

_____ iii. A Joint Government-Industry Effort

_____B. No. Not at this time.

_____C. Other Response: ______________________________

____

____

5. Should the U.S. consider developing a system of "Intelligent Software Agents" to detect suspicious transactional activity within Cyberpayment systems?

_____A. Yes. Such a System should be developed:

_____i. Independently by the U.S. Government

_____ ii. Collaboratively by the government and the Cyberpayment industry.

_____B. No. Not at this time.

_____C. Other Response: ______________________________

____

____

III. INTERNATIONAL CYBERPAYMENT ISSUES

The inherently international nature of many Cyberpayment products inhibits the effectiveness of any domestic law enforcement and regulatory response to patterns of abuse. The clear possibility exists that strong anti-Cyberpayment abuse regulations in the U.S. could be defeated by weak enforcement of similar rules in other countries. In this case, international consultations on Cyberpayment system oversight are advisable.

1. Should the U.S. continue to take an aggressive leadership role within the G-7/FATF framework on the basis that Cyberpayment systems could represent a weak link in US and global anti-money laundering efforts?

_____A. Yes. The U.S. should continue to seek to catalyze cooperative international efforts on Cyberpayment system oversight.

_____B. No. The U.S. Government should adopt a more hands off approach at this time to international Cyberpayment system oversight. The market can be relied upon to address potential fraud and abuse in deployed systems.

_____C. Other Response: ______________________________

____

____

IV. NEAR-TERM POLICY COORDINATION AND VULNERABILITY ANALYSIS

One of the important overarching issues in the Cyberpayments realm is how the U.S. Government should proceed in its analysis of potential Cyberpayment system vulnerabilities. In particular, is there now or might there at some point be a need for an Executive Branch agent with responsibilities and authority akin to that of the current so-called "drug czar" position.

1. Should the U.S. consider designating a senior Administration official as an Executive Agent responsible for coordinating information gathering and analysis of Cyberpayment system vulnerabilities?

   ______A. Yes.

   ______B. No, not at this time.

GLOSSARY

Active - X Control: A software component capable of independent data manipulation through a structured set of commands.

ADSL: Asymmetric Digital Subscriber Line - A protocol used to deliver high bandwidth communications over conventional copper wire telephone networks.

Bandwidth: The amount of data that can be sent through a given communications circuit per second.

Credit Cards -- Payment instruments that allow a user to pay for goods through funds credited to him/her by a credit card issuing company.

Cryptography -- The science and technology of keeping information secret from unauthorized parties by using a mathematical code or a cipher.

Debit Cards -- Payment instruments which, when used to pay for an item or gain access to cash, debit an funds-holding account at a financial institution up to the users available balance.

Denomination Limits -- The upper limit beyond which value can no longer be added to a Cyberpayment instrument - typically discussed in the context of Smart Cards.

Disintermediation -- The potential of Cyberpayments systems to allow "non-intermediated" transfers of value to take place without the involvement of an identifiable third party subject to legal and regulatory oversight.

Financial Action Task Force (FATF) -- The FATF is one of the key organizations that addresses the global problem of money laundering. Formed by the G-7 Economic Summit in 1989, the FATF is comprised of 26 countries, the European Commission and the Gulf Cooperation Council. It is dedicated to promoting the development of effective anti-money laundering controls and enhanced cooperation in counter-money laundering efforts among its members and around the world.

Financial Intelligence Unit (FIU) -- FIUs have been established in various countries around the world to detect criminal abuse of the financial system, ensure adherence to laws against financial crime and protect the banking community. FinCEN is one model of FIU and others exist in such countries as Great Britain, France, Belgium, the Netherlands, Argentina, and Australia. The Egmont group is an international organization formed in June 1995 by 24 countries and 8 international organizations and is comprised of FIUs from member states and international organizations interested in collaborating to combat money laundering.

FinCEN (Financial Crimes Enforcement Network) -- An agency of the U.S. Treasury Department established in 1990 by Treasury Order 105-08. FinCEN is a financial intelligence unit (FIU) specializing in anti-money laundering policy and regulatory coordination. FinCEN brings together government agencies and the private sector to identify ways to prevent and detect financial crime. It is responsible for administration of the Bank Secrecy Act under which domestic financial institutions are required to keep records and file reports of certain transactions and to implement anti-money laundering programs and compliance procedures.

Geographic Targeting Order (GTO) -- A legal order of limited duration issued by the Treasury Department under the Bank Secrecy Act (BSA) requiring a domestic financial institution or group of domestic financial institutions in a geographic area to maintain records or file reports, above and beyond the record-keeping requirements of the BSA, concerning certain specific transactions.

Global Information Infrastructure (GII) -- The term used to describe the convergence of local and wide area information networks fostered by the emergence of open standards in networks. Within the GII, common protocols allowing geographically separated dissimilar computer networks to interact with one another and exchange information (text, pictures, audio, or video) in a digital form. The redundant nature of the GII permits communications between networks to be routed around malfunctioning systems.

Integration -- The final phase of the three generic phases of money laundering where a criminal, having successfully concealed the origin of illicit proceeds, desires to use the money for legitimate financial purposes such as business or real estate purchases. To facilitate such transactions, the laundered funds may be integrated with money from legitimate commercial activities. The illicit funds thus take on the appearance of legitimacy.

Intelligent Software Agents -- Software programs designed to accomplish tasks independent of user intervention. In a network environment such programs may seek out patterns in a network traffic or in network usage by identifiable actors and aggregate this information into a structured presentation suitable for law enforcement use.

Internet Banking – The delivery of traditional banking services cover the Internet. Internet banking provides basic financial services such as funds transfers, bill paying and purchases of financial instruments to customers through an online connection.

Internet Gambling – The delivery of gaming opportunities through the Internet. These activities involve the playing of games of chance through a site of the world wide web, as well as the delivery of bookmaking services to gamblers connected through an online service.

ISDN: Integrated services digital Network - A hardware and software systems for the delivery of high bandwidth data communications over fiber optic networks.

Key Escrow -- Key Escrow encryption plans envision the use of a trusted agent or third party (governmental or non-governmental in nature) which would store an extra copy of a private key used in a Public-key encryption implementation. Under legal and administrative guidelines such a key would be made available to authorized agencies (e.g., Law Enforcement Agencies) for investigative purposes. With access to private keys, authorized agencies would be able to decrypt cyphertext (the encrypted information) containing potentially valuable data.

Key Recovery -- Key Recovery encryption plans envision the filing - by creators of encryption products - of plans for the recovery of private keys used in implementations of Public

Key encryption. Such recovery plans would be deposited with the Department of Justice, and would allow - under court order - Law Enforcement and other authorized government agencies to gain access to procedures and techniques which would allow the recovery of a private key used in a Public Key encryption system. This proposal originated after widespread criticism of earlier Key Escrow proposals. Specific implementations of Key Recovery have yet to be offered.

Layering -- The second phase of the three generic phases of money laundering where the criminal obscures the trail left by illicit proceeds (*aka* "dirty money"). The objective of this phase is to carry out a series of financial transactions in order to build layers between the funds and their illicit source. For example, a series of bank-to-bank wire transfers would constitute layering. Activities of this nature, especially when they involve funds transfers between tax haven and bank secrecy jurisdictions, make it very difficult for investigators to follow the trail of money.

Money Laundering -- The process of transforming the proceeds of illegal activities into legitimate tax-free capital. Another definition often cited is "the process by which one conceals the existence, legal source, or illegal application of income, and then disguises that income to make it appear legitimate."

Money Services Businesses (MSBs) – This term refers to a broad range of non-bank businesses that provide certain financial products to the public. MSBs include money transmitters, check cashiers, sellers and issuers of money orders and travelers checks, retail currency exchangers and providers of stored valued products.

Network Targeting Order (NTO) -- A postulated future legal order involving the utilization of network-borne Cyberpayment system control elements to interrogate stored value-type Smart Cards when they are used at a retail merchant or Cyberpayment issuer (financial institution or non-bank Cyberpayment firm) for value transfers.

Offshore: Foreign or overseas jurisdictions.

Payer Anonymity -- Smart Card and Internet-based payments systems allow a high degree of anonymity for the payer (or initiator) of transfers of value in a transaction. Anonymity may allow criminals to conceal their identities in Cyberpayments value transfers, thus facilitating money laundering. Restrictions on anonymity in SMARTCARD systems will assist law enforcement in tracking money laundering, but also involve difficult issues of privacy and security.

Peer-to-Peer Value Transfers -- Peer to Peer Value Transfers are a facility enabled by Smart Cards and Internet-based Cyberpayments systems that allows the holder of a Smart Card or Cyberpayments "wallet" to transfer some of its value to another Smart Card or Cyberpayments "wallet" holder. These value transfers are disintermediated, that is, they do not involve an identifiable third party subject to regulatory and law enforcement oversight.

Placement -- The initial phase of the three generic phases of money laundering where cash enters the financial system. For example, placement occurs when illicit cash is deposited in a bank or money orders are purchased using cash from a criminal enterprise. It is during the placement stage that illicit funds are most vulnerable to detection by law enforcement authorities.

Private-Key Encryption -- A system of encryption utilizing a single private key to both encrypt and decrypt messages. An example of a private key encryption standard is DES. Originally developed by the US Government, this algorithm lies at the center of many privately deployed encryption systems, including those used to protect electronic funds transfer systems.

Public Switched Network (PSN) -- the term commonly used in the U.S. telecommunications industry and elsewhere for the public telephone system.

Public-Key Encryption – A system of encryption utilizing a public key to authenticate the identity of an actor sending or receiving information through an encryption-enabled communications system. Public key encryption uses separate keys to encrypt and decrypt messages meant for an authorized user. The public key is widely distributed and is used to encrypt messages meant for the public key's legitimate holder. The holder (owner of the public key) can then decrypt a message using a secret private key secure in the knowledge that the message had not been altered in transit. Public key encryption systems also allow for the authentication of the identity of the sender in that they can be adjusted to include information regarding the identity of the sending party.

Purse Integrity -- The integrity of the "holder" of value contained within a Smart Card payment instrument. Because Smart Cards typically use a combined Public Key - Private Key encryption system to store value, these purses are subject to the vulnerabilities of established encryption systems.

Stale-dating of Smart Card Value -- A concept for manipulating the "aging" of stored value within Cyberpayment instruments for the purposes of regulatory and law enforcement oversight. In connection with an NTO, such a concept may assist governmental authorities in detecting criminal misuse of Cyberpayment systems.

Value Tagging -- A concept for tagging the value in a stored value instrument so that it can be tracked as it transits the Cyberpayment system.

MR-965-OSTP/FinCEN

ISBN 0-8330-2616-X

9 780833 026163 51500